A Trip To Freedom

A Trip To Freedom

How I used God's Word
to break the
Cycle of Abuse.

by
Ruth Johnson

Lighthouse of Hope Publications
Mill Creek, Washington

A TRIP TO FREEDOM
ISBN 0-9661470-0-6
Library of Congress Catalog Card Number: 97-80671
Copyright © 1997 by Lighthouse of Hope Publications

Published by:
Lighthouse of Hope Publications
914 164th Street SE, Suite 365
Mill Creek, Washington 98012
(425) 672-3698

Dedication

I dedicate this book to my children

*To Paul, whom I care about, so very much,
and I always will.*

*To Mary, who has overcome so much
and emerged from it all a beautiful person, whom
I am thankful and proud to have as my daughter.*

*To John, whose kindness, friendship and boundless zest for life
have enriched my life and inspired me and blessed
me in countless, wonderful ways.*

*I also dedicate this book to all the hurting men and women
who have found little or no lasting solutions to their pain from the glut
of psychology-based books that cram the self-help sections of secular
and Christian bookstores today. To these hurting men and women,
may "A Trip to Freedom" be a cup of cool, healing water for the barren
places in their souls.*

Table of Contents

Part One
Breaking the Cycle of Abuse: The First Step

Part Two
Facing the Past

Part Three
Facing the Present: The changes I need to make.

Acknowledgements

Thank you, Ron Kamys, for inspiring the title to this book, when you shared that "reading it was a trip to freedom." I appreciate all your honesty and encouragement.

Thank you, to my daughter, Mary, for all your supportive help with the final work on "A Trip to Freedom." I pray that your moving story and the miracle God's restoration in your life truly will touch many lives.

Thank you Lola Clarke, Donna Stuart, Phadrae Halfacre and Linda D'Avola for all your encouragement in what God has called me to be. You have each touched my life in a profound and deeply appreciated way.

My heartfelt gratitude, to Nick and Sheila Stark, for making the publication of this book possible. Thank you for believing, so wholeheartedly, that God wants to use this book to bring revelation and healing into countless lives. May God bless you both for your "bread cast upon the waters" and your faithful friendship to me and my husband as we fulfill our calling to serve Him.

Introduction

For sixteen years I carefully recorded every revelation God gave me into how to break the cycle of abuse in my life. This book contains the keys that opened the door into that transformation. If you are looking, as I once did, for the answers to end your treadmill of abusive relationships, the revelations in this book can truly be your "trip to freedom". I was forty-seven years old before my life-long pattern of being drawn to abusive relationships was finally over. It is my earnest prayer that anyone reading this book will not have to take as long as I did to experience that breakthrough.

For the sake of brevity, "he" is used, throughout this book, to refer to the person who is abusive. In all instances, the "he" could be either a man or a woman.

Part One

Breaking the Cycle of Abuse:

The First Step

Chapter One

I need Jesus!

Every person has a basic need to give and receive love. However, too often people choose relationships in which this healthy exchange of love is not possible. If I am one of those people, I might even tell myself,

"Never again am I going to get involved with someone who is emotionally incapable of loving me or of receiving my love for him! Never again am I going to let someone abuse me!"

Yet, I do what I promised myself I would not do. I end up in another destructive relationship.

Until I was forty-seven years old, I was entrenched in this cycle of repeatedly choosing abusive relationships. Today, all that has changed!

My life is rich with healthy, rewarding, mutually supportive relationships. The people I am close to are nothing like the ones of the past, who inflicted so much pain. Only God could empower me with the courage to end my attraction to painful relationships and to confront, honestly, those that were abusive.

In the chapters that follow, I share the Biblically based insights He gave me that equipped me to make that remarkable transition. I explain the *"breathtaking recovery life makes in anyone who grasps with both hands the wildly extravagant life-gift, the grand setting-everything-right that Jesus provides" (Romans Chapter Five The Message Personalized).*

The catalyst for that breathtaking recovery was God's Word. Through the truth in His Word, God *"set my heart free" (Psalm 119:32 NIV).*

However, before any Scripture could have this profound impact on my life, I had to take the first step. I had to find Jesus.

* * *

My journey in search of Him began as a young child.

I was the third of five children in an Irish Catholic family. We lived in a cold water tenement in a slum in South Boston, Massachusetts. Through the dirty living-room window, I could see towering mounds of black coal in the old factory across the street. Aging buses sat idle in the run-down bus barn on the opposite corner.

Growing up, our family was not close. We never did things together. Though we were all hurting, we didn't talk about our feelings. My brothers and sisters and I withdrew from each other into our separate worlds. We remained distant, even during the hard times. We did not help each other.

My first troubling memory occurred when I was five years old. It was the day I began kindergarten. I was excited about starting school, but I was also uneasy. It was a long way from home. I had never been that far by myself.

"Mama will go with me," I comforted myself, as I watched my older brother and sister leave without me. I gulped down breakfast and quickly put on my uniform. Dressed and eager to go, I sat on the edge of the frayed, brown couch in the livingroom. I waited, anxiously, for Mom to appear.

"I'm not going with you," she eventually yelled from her bedroom.

"But Mom, I don't know my way. Please come with me," I pleaded, as I walked quickly towards her room. "I'm scared to go by myself!"

"I don't feel good," she responded, coldly, as she shut the door. "You'll have to go alone."

At that point, I realized I could not convince my mother to change her mind. I stood outside her closed bedroom door and shuddered at the thought of finding my way on my own. Yet, I did not want to miss out on the first day of kindergarten. After a long silence, I forced myself to leave. I walked briskly down the street away from our home. When I could no longer see our house, I ran as fast as I could. I kept running, faster and faster, until it hurt to breathe.

"I hope I don't get lost," I kept telling myself, in a panic.

Finally, I turned a corner and there was St. Mark's School up ahead. I slowed my pace to catch my breath.

The closer I walked to the front entrance, the more nervous I became. I hoped to catch a glimpse of my older brother and sister, but they were nowhere in sight. I tentatively approached the school office and was relieved when an older nun motioned to me· to follow her. Moments later, she left me standing at the open door of a crowded classroom. I looked around at all the new faces. Many of the children were crying and clinging to their mothers.

My eyes puddled with tears.

"I wish Mom was here," I said to myself. Hot tears rolled down my cheeks. "I wish her arms were around me. I'd feel so much better."

I stood and stared, forlornly, at the other children for what seemed like a long, long time. Eventually, a young nun settled us in our seats. All the mothers waved goodbye and left. Somehow I survived that first day of kindergarten, but the sadness I felt never left me.

There were many other troubling times with Mom. One of the most difficult was the evening meal. It was the only time everyone in our family was together. We ate in tense silence. Mom sat stiffly at the head of the old, wooden table. She positioned her tightly clenched fists on both sides of her plate.

"Shut up!" Mom yelled, if one of us kids made the slightest noise.

I winced at the sound of her shrill voice.   Inevitably, my stomach ached. Every night, I could hardly wait for the meal to end so that I could retreat into the solace of my room.

After dinner, Mom usually stayed alone in the kitchen. She leaned over the sink and buried her face in her folded arms. She moaned with pain. I wanted so much to put my arms around her and comfort her. One night, I approached her.

"Mom, are you all right?" I said, as I walked, uncertainly, into the kitchen. "Mom, is there anything I can ...."

"Get out of here!" she screamed, before I could finish speaking.

I hesitated. "But Mom...."

"Shut up and get out of here," she yelled, as she whirled around and glared at me. "Leave me alone!"

I did leave her alone, but I ached inside because I could never show her that I cared.

Mom became increasingly more despondent as I grew older. Late one afternoon, my mother and I were home alone. From my bedroom, I suddenly heard loud weeping. I rushed into the kitchen. Mom was sprawled on the floor, crying hysterically.

"What's wrong?" I asked, with alarm. "Please, tell me what's wrong!" She shook her head and kept crying, uncontrollably.

"Please talk to me," I pleaded with her, as I put my hand gently on her shoulder. She couldn't speak.

I ran to a neighbor's house and banged, loudly, on the front door. Minutes later, I heard the shrill of sirens. An ambulance stopped at our house. Two men in white jackets ran into the kitchen, strapped Mom to a stretcher and took her away.

No one in our family talked about what happened to my mother that day. This silence made her leaving me all the more distressing. I wondered if she would ever come back.

Eventually, she did, but I could tell she was even sadder. Now, she often lay in her bed all day long. A cold, wet washcloth covered her eyes. Mom hated sunlight, so our house was kept dark. Every shade was pulled down tight against the windowsills. Tattered, heavy drapes were always kept closed to block out any daylight.

"Maybe, today, Mom and I can spend some time together," I often said to myself, on the way home from school. "Maybe today she'll be all right."

But Mom was never all right.

"Leave me alone," she screamed at me almost every afternoon, as soon as I walked into the house from school.

"Get out of here and leave me alone," she shrieked, if I ever tried to say hello to her. "And don't make any noise. I want it quiet."

I could hardly wait for the days she walked to the grocery store. As soon as she disappeared around the corner, I pulled up all the shades. I happily opened the windows. Cheery sunlight instantly flooded our home. I sang and sang, the entire time she was gone. When I heard Mom walking up the steps of the front porch, I immediately stopped singing. I rushed to close the windows and pull down the shades. My world went dark again.

My relationship with my father was equally disturbing.

He was a tall man with bright blue eyes that had a lighthearted twinkle. When Pop took me places, that was the only time I went anywhere fun. Any laughter or warmth that was in our home, it came from Pop. He loved to sing, play pretty music, bake homemade bread and make his own blackberry jam. I loved it when his bread came hot out of the oven and we smeared it with his fresh jam.

Yet, it hurt to love Pop. I never knew when he would disappear. I didn't know where he went or how long he would be away. He never said good-bye. While he was gone, the one bright spot in our home left as well. It was as if the lights went out in our family.

My father had a stormy relationship with my older sister.

I tried harder and harder to be good in order to gain Pop's approval, but my older sister didn't care. She was always getting in trouble. By the time she started high school, my parents couldn't control her.

Late one evening, I heard her angry screams coming from their bedroom. I jumped up from my chair and ran to their room. Mom was forcing my sister to lay on the bed, while Pop beat her all over her body with his thick leather belt.

"Stop," I begged, in a loud, desperate voice from where I stood in the doorway. "Please, please stop!"

They ignored my pleas. Pop hit my sister, over and over, while I sobbed nearby. A year later she was taken from our home and placed in an institution for teenage girls. She never came back to live with us.

In the midst of all this unhappiness, I began a close friendship with God. I didn't know about Jesus, but through my Catholic upbringing, I knew about God. From a young age, I talked to Him about everything. The only time life made any sense was when I was with Him. This friendship was my only refuge from my troubled feelings. It was my only comfort in an otherwise lonely childhood.

At times, I longed for someone to hold me and hug me, but there was no affection in our family. My relationship with Pop was no exception. Although I loved him, I became keenly aware of the distance between us by the time I was in eighth grade. In an effort to get closer to him, I decided to start a new bedtime tradition. I would kiss him on the cheek and hug him every night before I went to bed.

Being affectionate with Pop felt awkward at first. It was uncomfortable for my father as well. He flinched and pulled back from me the first time I kissed him on the cheek. I refused to let his revulsion deter me. I made up my mind, "Even if Pop doesn't return my affection, I will still give mine to him." For me, showing Pop I loved him was better than no one in the family ever showing love towards anyone at all.

Despite this effort, I harbored a confusing anger towards my father. Late one evening, it exploded in a fit of rage.

"I hate you, Pop!" I screamed at him, as I stood facing him in the middle of our livingroom. "I hate you!"

My father didn't say a word. He stared at me, with a silent agony in his eyes, as if to say, "I deserve to be hated."

My outburst ended. Pop quietly walked away from me, his shoulders stooped over like those of a broken, defeated man. I immediately regretted hurting him. I never wanted to hate my father. I needed him. I needed his love. I wanted more than anything in the world to be close to him, but I could not bridge the dark, widening chasm between us.

My friendship with God became more and more important to me. I felt a growing desire to dedicate my life to serving the only Person who ever loved me! The only possible way to fulfill that desire, as a young Catholic girl, was to become a Nun.

When I became a freshman at Notre Dame Academy, I decided that some day I would enter the convent. Throughout my years in high school, my thoughts and plans centered on that goal. "As soon as I graduate," I promised myself, "I will become a Dominican Sister."

A month after my graduation, the keenly anticipated day to leave for the convent finally arrived.

Pop's health was too weak for him to make the trip with me. Without a word, I hugged him goodbye and slowly walked down the steps to the car.

Tears blurred my vision, as I looked back over my shoulder at Pop. He stood on the same weather-beaten porch where I had spent so many hours alone as a little girl. I riveted my eyes on my father and waved to him through the back window. An overwhelming sadness engulfed me as soon as he disappeared from view. I never really knew Pop. Now, abruptly, my life with him was ending. Once I entered the convent, I could not come back home to see him. Our time together, as father and daughter, was over.

I hurriedly wiped away my tears and turned my focus to what was ahead of me.

"I have a new life to look forward to, now," I told myself, confidently. "Everything's going to be all right."

Two hours later, we drove into the long, graveled driveway of the Dominican Monastery. I was in awe of the peaceful beauty of the grounds. The walkways were meticulously landscaped. Tall eucalyptus trees towered against the late afternoon sky. The only sounds I heard, when the car motor stopped, were the chirps of the birds in the branches overhead.

"Surely here I will be happy," I told myself, reassuringly, as I looked around with amazement at my new home.

We walked up a long flight of freshly painted steps and knocked on the huge wooden door. An older nun slowly opened it. She immediately motioned to my family to wait for me in an austerely furnished parlor. Then she briskly ushered me into another room and pointed to my new clothes.

When I rejoined my family, I was dressed in black. My hair was hidden under the short, black veil of a Postulant.

Moments later, I said goodbye to Mom and my brothers and sisters. I brimmed with excitement and anticipation. The heavy door closed behind them. I now was cloistered from the rest of the world. From that moment, I was in total obedience to Mother Superior. I was bound by the strict rules of the Dominicans.

My giddy excitement faded quickly. By the second week, I was deeply affected by being abruptly cut off from my family. I missed Mom and Pop and my brothers and sisters. No matter how miserable life had been at home, they were my family. They were my roots. They were all I had. I cried every time I thought about them.

At night, I tossed and turned, restlessly, in bed. I paced the dark halls of the old monastery, until I was weary enough to sleep. My loneliness was unbearable. Though I was unhappy, I decided to stay. I had learned a new concept about God, since becoming a Postulant. He wanted me to do His will, no matter how much I must suffer to obey Him. I was now taught on a daily basis that the more I suffered, the more I demonstrated my love for Him.

After six months, I became a Novice. My name was changed to Sister Naomi. My hair was cropped short and hidden under a long, white veil. I dedicated myself to the life of a Nun. I lived in silence, except for a brief, designated time in the afternoon. I spent hours, each day, saying my prayers in Latin and singing the Gregorian Chants with the other young Nuns in the Chapel. Yet, no matter how hard I tried to do everything I was required to do, I was troubled.

"God, please help me," I often prayed, as I knelt alone in the chapel late at night.

"I'm confused, Lord. I feel so alone. You seem farther and farther away from me."

I paused and watched the many votive lights flickering in the dark shadows of the chapel.

"All I've ever wanted was to serve you. I want more than anything in the world to do your will. I'll do whatever you want me to do, but what are you asking of me?"

I prayed and listened, night after night, but there was no answer. I had no peace. My private agony continued.

All the comfort I received from talking to God as a child was now gone. I had a difficult time feeling close to someone who wanted me to hurt so deeply in order to serve Him.

I wanted to run far away. I longed to find a place I could be happy, but I could not leave. If I did, I was now convinced that I would be turning my back on God. I couldn't stand the thought of living with the guilt of that decision.

After a year and a half, I made public vows of poverty, chastity and obedience for three years. I exchanged the white veil for a black one. With a heavy heart, I accepted my unhappiness as the suffering I must endure to serve God.

Meanwhile, Pop's health worsened. He became severely depressed and tried to kill himself. He was then committed to a state mental hospital and put under close observation. Unexpectedly, Mother Superior gave me permission to visit him.

Pop's eyes flickered with recognition, when I walked into his dimly lit room. I stood, quietly, by his bed, as he lapsed in and out of consciousness. His gaunt face was ashen with the pallor of imminent death. Despite his weakened condition, he was very much aware that I was with him. He held on tight to my hand and never let it go.

Tears stung my cheeks, as the years with Pop flashed before me. Ever since I left home for the convent, he tried to show me that he loved me. He sent me long, encouraging letters, hand painted cards and poems he wrote about us. In his own way, Pop said he was sorry for failing me as a father.

I stared at him, sadly, and reflected on the one time that I told him I hated him. I still regretted those cruel words.

"Pop, I didn't hate you," I ached to say to him. "I'm so sorry I said that to you. I love you, Pop. I really do...."

I left him, that day, without ever speaking those words. He died the next morning.

Inconsolable grief gripped me.

I wept for the loss of a relationship with my father that now would never be possible. I couldn't forgive myself for not telling him I was sorry and that I loved him the last time I was with him.

My turmoil as a Nun intensified.

I wrestled with an agonizing guilt, whenever I considered leaving the convent. Even if I ever felt free to leave, I was overcome with fear at any thought of launching out on my own and starting a new life. Nonetheless, I finally accepted I could not make the vows of a Nun for life. I decided to leave the week before I had to be in a ceremony to make that commitment.

Once I made this decision, I comforted myself with the thought, "Soon I will be back home. I will have my family to stay with. I won't be completely on my own."

I had rarely seen Mom and my brothers and sisters since entering the convent. Now, I ached to know that they cared about me.

The day of my departure finally arrived. After the morning prayers, I quickly left the chapel. Sister Superior took me to a room where she directed me to change into the clothes Mom brought to me.

With mixed feelings, I slowly removed the long, black veil from my head for the last time. I placed it, carefully, on the bed.

"I wonder what the future will hold for me, now," I asked myself, as I stared, pensively, into the full-length mirror. Gone was the girl of eighteen, who was so young, so hopeful, so full of dreams of a happy, new life. The woman I saw reflected in the mirror was a stranger to me.

Uncertainty wrinkled my brow. I had been hidden away from television and newspapers. I had no understanding of the many ways the world had changed. The cloistered convent was the only home I had known for five years.

I sighed, finished getting dressed and walked out into the dark hallway. With mixed emotions, I descended the long flight of stairs that led to the front door below. Several nuns waited at the bottom of the stairs to say goodbye to me. Each one hugged me warmly, with much concern in their eyes.

"Are you absolutely sure, Sister Naomi, that you have to leave us?" my favorite older nun asked me, as she held me in her arms and cried. "Yes, Sister," I assured her. "I must go."

I turned away from her and hurried out the door into the waiting car. I never looked back.

"Maybe now that I'm older things will be different at home," I told myself, hopefully, during the long, silent ride back to where I used to live. "Maybe, now, we can be close."

Home wasn't different.

My brothers and sisters were even more distant towards me than when we were growing up. They had no room for me in their new lives. Mom didn't want me around either. Within days, the loneliness returned that tormented me as a child.

After I lived with Mom two weeks, she pressured me to move out. I had no money, no friends, no car, no clothes of my own and no job. Worst of all, I had to face, once again, that I had no family. I needed a place of safety and support to reestablish my life. Instead, I was forced to face the harsh reality that I didn't have the home to come back to that I had dreamed about during my final weeks in the convent.

I found a low paying teaching position in a Catholic grammar school that I could get to by bus. With my first paycheck, I moved into an inexpensive apartment, far from the town where Mom lived.

My life immediately spun out of control.

I couldn't talk to God anymore. I had given Him the best years of my youth, only to have my dream to serve Him crushed. I felt betrayed by the Person I had paid such a dear price to love.

I began to drink heavily to escape the frightening chaos churning inside of me. The only way I could block out the pain was to pass out drunk each night and fall asleep.

Within a few months, I invited different men into my apartment to stay the night. The gnawing emptiness inside of me plunged me into a darker and darker abyss.

During this tumultuous time, I met an older man. Jim was charming and attentive. He said all the words I always wanted a man to say to me. From the first night I met him, we spent every possible moment together. He drank heavily, but I was oblivious to the seriousness of his drinking problem.

There was an even darker side to his personality.

Late one Saturday morning, we sat at my kitchen table. I leisurely watched my gray, fuzzy kitten playfully chase a ball of yarn across the carpet. Innocently, the kitten stopped and urinated. Jim suddenly jumped up from his chair. He yelled obscenities, as he rushed towards the unsuspecting kitten. He grabbed it around its soft belly and squeezed it with all his strength.

The kitten's paws flailed, helplessly, in the air. It writhed and moaned with pain.

Jim took off his thick leather belt. I watched, in horror, as he knelt down. He forced the frantic kitten to stay on the floor and brutally beat it with the belt.

"Stop! Stop!" I yelled. The kitten struggled to escape from Jim's iron grip, its eyes pitifully wild with fright.

"Stop!" I screamed, even louder. Jim hurled the terror-stricken kitten across the room. It limped to a place of safety under the bed.

"Why did you do that"! I demanded.

"I hate cats," he muttered, breathing heavily.

Moments later, I agreed to let him get rid of the kitten to avoid any further problems. He took it with him when he left to go home.

"I threw that damn cat off a bridge into the river," he bragged, with a sinister, scary look in his eyes, the next time I saw him.

I felt uneasy, but I pushed Jim's violent behavior out of my mind. I quickly dismissed it as having nothing to do with our relationship. It never occurred to me that the brutal rage he inflicted on that helpless kitten could some day be unleashed on me!

Not long after Jim moved into my apartment, he stopped talking to me. He ignored any of my efforts to be close to him. His attentiveness towards me ended.

Early one summer evening, I lay stiffly by his side in bed.

"I miss the way we used to talk," I said, hoping he would respond.

"Please talk to me," I pleaded.

He turned his back to me and ignored my efforts to get him to speak to me. Moments later, I got out of bed, hurt by his coldness.

"You used to like to talk to me," I continued.

I became increasingly more agitated, as I glared at him lying there in stony silence.

"I don't understand what's happening between us...."

With no warning, Jim leaped angrily out of bed. He pinned me against the wall. I was stunned. His large hand came at me. I futilely covered my face and head with my arms, as he punched me, over and over. My head wrenched from side to side, with each forceful blow.

"Stop," I screamed, hysterically. "Please stop," I begged him.

Jim ignored my pleas. Then, just as suddenly as his rage had begun, it ended. I slumped to the floor. My bruised body went limp. I gasped for air, as he walked away from me and sullenly went back to bed. After that night, I did not relax when I was around him.

Despite this alarming incident and Jim's refusal to communicate with me, I still married him. Then began a reign of terror. I lived each day wondering if he would attack me. Fear became a way of life.

Prescription drugs numbed my pain. I drank earlier and earlier in the morning to muster up the strength to face each day.

To hide my husband's abuse, I didn't let people get close to me. I was too ashamed to let anyone know what was really going on in our marriage. That withdrawal kept me dangerously isolated. I slipped deeper and deeper into a suicidal despair.

Six tortuous years passed. I hated my husband. Even more passionately, I hated Mom. Searing memories of all the ways she had hurt me dominated my thoughts. I constantly relived each painful incident in my mind.

One bleak afternoon, I stared, wearily, out of the second story window of our damp, dimly lit apartment. The dark winter sky cast an ominous gray pallor over the deserted street below. I was thirty years old and I wanted to die. I hadn't talked to God in many years, but I had no one else to turn to.

"God, please help me," I whispered, tentatively at first. "I beg you, please help me!"

I pressed my forehead against the cold windowpane and shivered from the chill.

"I used to be so close to You when I was a little girl," I continued, hoarsely, through my tears. "You were all I had. I don't know when I lost you. But, God, I need you now. I beg you, be real to me now."

I hid my face in my trembling hands to muffle my sobs, but I could not contain the explosive emotions convulsing on the inside of me.

"If you don't help me," I cried out, in a loud, desperate voice, "I don't want to live any longer. I feel too lost, too scared. Please....please help me..."

At that moment, God's Presence filled the room. It was the same Presence that I knew so well as a child. My sobs subsided. I knelt in hushed awe. I hungrily soaked up the comfort of the kind, gentle Presence that surrounded me.

"Ruth, I hear your cries," God assured me in my heart. "I'm right here and I'm going to help you. I've wanted to help you all along, but I've been waiting for you to come to me and let me be close to you once again."

"Oh God," I prayed aloud, my voice choked with emotion. "It's You. It's really You! It's been such a long, long time since I have felt close to you. I thought I had lost you, forever. I've missed you so much."

"I'm going to show you where to find Me," He continued to tell me. "I will take you by the hand and show you the way. Search for Me and you will find Me."

Then, just as suddenly as He had come, God's Presence left. I knelt, for a long time, and reflected on His last words to me, "Search for Me and you will find Me."

Hope stirred within me. A new resolve flooded my soul. I would not rest until I found that Presence again.

I visited numerous churches of many denominations. Six months went by. My search continued. Finally, one Sunday morning, I found Him. I walked into a small church. The pastor was preaching on the story of Naomi and Ruth.

"God loved Ruth," he explained, compassionately, as I sat down in a wooden pew at the back of the church.

"He wanted to protect Naomi. He wanted to take care of her every need."

Tears instantly streamed down my face. "Oh God," I prayed. "No one here knows me. This pastor has no idea that my name is Ruth. He doesn't know that my name in the convent was Sister Naomi. Only you know this. You gave him this sermon for me. You love me. You really do."

God's kind, caring love for me flooded my weary soul. The minute the pastor asked if anyone wanted to be saved, I went quickly to the front of the church. I gratefully accepted Jesus as my personal Savior.

"I open myself up to you, completely," I told the Lord, as I knelt at the altar. "I surrender all to you, Jesus. I want all you have for me!"

I lingered there, for a long time. A healing, soothing peace enveloped me. For the first time in many years, I felt myself relax.

When I left the church that day, the loneliness that had preyed on my mind, since I was a child, was gone. The Presence of God that I had searched for was now in my heart to stay. All I had ever wanted was to have someone love me. Now, I was restored to the only Person who had ever given me that love. I knew I would not walk away from Him again!

"Now I understand what was missing all these years," I reflected, as I drove home.

"I loved you growing up, Lord. I wanted to serve you with all of my heart in the convent, but I didn't know Jesus. I could talk to you, but You couldn't be close to me the way You really wanted to be. You couldn't, because You didn't live on the inside of me. And I had no understanding of Your Word, so I was truly, truly lost."

I later found two Scriptures that describe what happened to me that unforgettable day...

"I wandered for years in the desert, looking but not finding a good place to live, half starved and parched with thirst, staggering and stumbling on the brink of exhaustion. Then in my desperate condition I called out to God. He got me out in the nick of time.

He put my feet on a wonderful road that took me straight to a good place to live in Him. I thank God for His marvelous love, His miracle mercy to me, whom He loves."

"He caught me. He reached all the way from sky to sea. He pulled me out of my ocean of hate, that enemy chaos, the void in which I was drowning. Others hit me when I was down, but God stuck by me. He stood me up on a wide-open field. I stood there saved – surprised to be loved! He made my life complete as soon as I placed all the pieces before Him. He gave me a fresh start!"

* * *

All dependency on drugs and drinking ended the day I found Jesus. My life immediately took on a new purpose. I experienced a renewed passion to serve the Lord I had so longed to serve since I was a young child.

I also had high hopes that getting saved would begin the healing process in my marriage. Instead, Jim despised my new love for Jesus. His attacks escalated. I became increasingly more frightened by his violent outbursts of anger.

One Saturday morning, toward the end of my first year as a Christian, my two young children sat at the kitchen table. They listened in tense silence to my husband and me argue.

Without warning he lunged at me. He furiously wrapped his hands around my neck and dragged me across the kitchen floor.

"I'm going to kill you!" he screamed, as he brutally squeezed my neck, tighter and tighter.

I panicked. I gasped for air. My arms thrashed, convulsively. I grabbed at his hands as I frantically tried to wrench free from his grip. Then, suddenly, I went limp in his hands. I was too petrified to fight back. Only with my terrified eyes could I beg him to stop!

Seconds later he threw me, roughly, to the floor. His hands were clenched in tight fists at his side as he stormed out of the room.

The children crept quietly away from the kitchen table. They took refuge in their rooms, too scared to speak or even look at me.

For the remainder of that weekend, I lived every moment with a paralyzing fear.

"What if he turns on me again!" I kept saying to myself in a frenzy. "What if I say the wrong thing and he tries to strangle me again? The next time he might kill me!"

I waited for the first opportunity to escape with my children! Monday morning, he left for work. As soon as his car disappeared from view, I left him.

It took many years of physical therapy and persistent prayer before I was free of severe, constant pain caused by the injury to my neck. My emotional scars took even longer to heal.

Finding Jesus was my first step towards that healing. However, there was much that I had to learn before I was set free of the damage from my past.

I tried to find happiness, when my marriage ended. Instead, I chose a disheartening detour. I rushed into another abusive marriage. For the next fourteen years of this destructive relationship, God exposed layers of twisted thinking that had been ingrained in me since early childhood. I struggled with the consequences of my mistakes, but God never gave up on me.

Every time I chose a direction that made it difficult for Him to help me, He extended His mercy to me. He reached down and picked me up. He helped me find my way back to the place I needed to be, so that He could continue healing me.

Today, my endless detours into sick relationships are over. I am free!

Yet, *God "doesn't show partiality" (Acts 10:34 NLT).*   What He has done for me, He wants to do for anyone who cries out to Him for help. He speaks these words of hope to every person who is still imprisoned in the shackles of abuse, as I once was...

*"I want to rescue you from dead-end alleys
and dark dungeons.*

*I want to set you up in the kingdom of My Son,
whom I love so much,*

The Son who can get you out of the pit you are in,

*who can get rid of the sins
you are doomed to keep repeating."*

*(Colossians Chapter One The Message)
Personalized*

"It makes no difference who you are or where you are from.

If you want Me and are ready to do as I say,

the door is open."

*(Acts Chapter Ten The Message)
Personalized*

Part Two

Facing the Past

God warns us:

"My people are destroyed for lack of knowledge."
(Hosea 4:6 NAS)

**His provision to protect us from that
destruction is the truth!**

"The truth shall make you free."
(John 8:32 NAS)

Therefore, the beginning of being set free from the cycle of
abuse is to gain an understanding of the root causes for that pattern
of choosing sick relationships.

**Part Two explores some of these
common issues.**

Chapter Two

A healthy relationship is reciprocal!

**To establish healthy relationships,
I must never lose sight of the following truth:**

An intimate relationship must be reciprocal.

Therefore, it is no longer acceptable for me to do all of the caring, all of the giving, all of the helping in a relationship with a spouse or a close friend. If I interact in that way in an intimate relationship, I have become a caretaker or parent to my spouse or friend. I have taken on too much responsibility for the other person's needs. In doing so, I have relinquished a healthy consideration of my own.

Healthy love is a "mutual give and take".

It is not: "I give. I bend. I accommodate your needs and wishes and you can do all of the taking!" Unfortunately, as a child, that is exactly how I learned to define love.

I couldn't stand to see everyone hurting in my family. I gave and gave and gave to each of them. I dared not hope to be loved in return. That expectation was futile, since no one in my family could reciprocate my love. I decided, as young as late grammar school, it was better for me to show my family I loved them, even if no one loved me back. To me, love going in one direction was better than no one loving anyone at all.

That decision set a pattern for all my future relationships. Abusive men were drawn to my willingness to give them so much and expect so very little in return for myself.

Once I understood how unhealthy this pattern of behavior was, I realized that I had to remind myself, often:

A healthy person is not comfortable with being a 'taker' in a relationship and letting me do most of the giving.

The Word of God stresses this reciprocal nature of a healthy relationship. The Scriptures make it clear that loving, giving, encouraging and caring are to be *"one to another"* and not just me doing all of that for my spouse or close friend:

"Serve one another."
(Galatians 5:13 NAS)

"Accept one another."
(Romans 15:7 NAS)

"Encourage each other."
(II Corinthians 13:11 NLT)

"Love each other with genuine affection, and take delight in honoring each other."
(Romans 12:10 NLT)

"Have the same care for one another."
(I Corinthians 12:25 NAS)

The Word makes it clear that, even in the spiritual realm, even for the Apostle Paul, an intimate relationship needs to be mutually supportive:

"I'm eager to encourage you in your faith, but I also want to be encouraged by yours. In this way, each of us will be a blessing to the other" *(Romans 1:12 NLT).*

Chapter Three

Behaviors, not words, tell the truth!

To stop my attraction to destructive relationships...

I must be a "behavior observer"!
That is the only way I can determine
the truth about a person.

From a young age, my relationship with my mother reinforced in me the opposite reality.

"Ruth, I love you," she occasionally told me. However, her words never matched her cold, rejecting behaviors. At my slightest reluctance to believe her words, she added, convincingly, "You know I do!" I then felt required to accept that, if she said she loved me, I had to believe her, no matter how she treated me. As I grew older, I took this conditioning into my relationships with men.

When both of the abusive men I eventually married told me, "Ruth, I love you," I accepted their words as the truth. It never occurred to me to watch their behaviors to verify the validity of what they said to me. Hearing them tell me, "I love you", was enough for me. I expected and looked for nothing more.

When I became determined to stop my attraction to abusive men, I realized that I could never again be so foolishly, blindly trusting. I could not accept a person's words, independent of what he communicates to me through his behaviors.

To protect myself from falling back into the familiar way of thinking that always propelled me towards damaging relationships, I reminded myself, often, of God's warning:

> *"Violent people deceive their companions,*
> *leading them down a harmful path!"*
> *(Proverbs 16:29 NLT)*

In other words...

Abusive, controlling, unhealthy people are frequently excellent talkers, who are highly skilled in the art of manipulation in relationships. However, if I carefully observe their behaviors, I will see that their actions do not match their words.

"Actions speak louder than words" is a common saying.

God's Word makes this same point,
clearly and unequivocally!

> *"Let us stop just saying we love each other;*
> *let us really show it by our actions.*
> *It is by our actions that we know we are living in the truth..."*
> *(I John 3:18-19 NLT)*

> *"Who (people) are is the main thing, not what they say."*
> *(Matthew Chapter Seven The Message)*
> *Personalized*

> *"Doing, not hearing (i.e. not just words!),*
> *is what makes the difference with God."*
> *(Romans Chapter Two The Message)*

> *"It's the way you live, not the way you talk, that counts!"*
> *(James Chapter Three The Message)*

Chapter Four

Normal is not supposed to mean pain!

**If you have a history of abusive relationships,
you need to remind yourself, often:**

It is not normal to be in constant emotional pain.

It is not normal to be neglected or treated with verbal,
physical, mental or emotional cruelty! Yet, in my family, I was
conditioned to see these behaviors as the way life is. I never knew it
could be any different.

I lived with an emotional pain that never went away, as I
grew up. I was also forced to watch my brothers and sisters hurt.
Their suffering was far more upsetting to me than anything that was
done to me. I felt terribly distraught, whenever one of them was
being mistreated and I was helpless to intervene and stop the abuse.
Consequently, when I met my first husband, I did not know what it
even meant to be loved or treated with kindness. I had no idea what
it felt like to be happy or to observe someone else feeling happy.
Consequently, I brought into this relationship a warped acceptance of
emotional pain.

I lived with Jim for a year before I married him. During that
time, he abused me physically, emotionally, verbally and even
sexually. Yet, I stayed with him. No warning bells went off inside
me, telling me:

"Something is really sick, really wrong with this relationship.
I need to end it immediately!"

Quite the opposite!

I accepted this man's indifference to my feelings. I was frightened by his rage, but I did not consider leaving him. Despite his cruel behaviors, I married him! In doing so, I moved into familiar territory. Normal, once again, meant I was constantly hurting.

Only after many years as a Christian did I recognize how unhealthy I was in my high tolerance for emotional pain. When I studied God's Word, over a long period of time, I finally grasped this Biblical truth:

**God doesn't want me to accept
being mistreated in any relationship.
In fact, He calls abusive people wicked:**

"The wicked are sewers of abuse!"
(Proverbs Chapter Fifteen   The Message)

**He tells me not to even associate
with abusive people!**

*"You are not to associate with anyone
who claims to be a Christian, yet is abusive…
Don't even eat with such people!"*
(I Corinthians 5:11 NLT)

The longer I walked with Jesus, the more I understood:
He not only does not want me to accept being abused,
He does not want me to *"lack **any** good thing."*
(Psalm 34:9-10 NLT)

Contrary to all that I had ever experienced,
His *"purpose is to give me life in **all** its fullness!"*
(John 10:10 NLT)
Personalized

His desire for me, and each one of His children, is to bless and prosper us *"infinitely more than we would ever dare to ask or hope" (Ephesians 3:20 NLT)*.

Accepting, as normal, the emotionally crippling pain of an abusive relationship, definitely is *not "life in all its fullness."* Most assuredly, it is not the fulfillment of *"infinitely more than I would ever dare to ask my 'Abba Father' for or hope that He would give me."*

Chapter Five

I need a "Dad"!

If I didn't have a Mom or Dad who loved me the way I needed, as a child, I am left with a giant void. I will never be completely free of the damage from that loss, unless my need for the love of a father and mother is met. I can't look to my earthly parents to provide that love. They may never be able to. My becoming whole cannot depend on them.

Only God can fill this empty place in my soul. If He doesn't, I remain stuck in the cycle of abuse. In close relationships, I am drawn to what is familiar. I am attracted to people who mistreat me in the same way that I suffered as a child. I recreate, especially with a spouse, the same destructive behaviors that I was accustomed to experiencing with the parent who abused me.

Inevitably, I wake up one day, in a marriage, and realize, "This person is just like my Mom or Dad!"

In this chapter and the following one, I explain how God's love can fill the need for the love of a father and mother. Through poignant, powerful Scriptures, God reveals Himself as a very real "Dad" and the provider of a mother's comforting, nurturing love. In His own tender words, God expresses His heart to His hurting children. He makes it clear, over and over, that He yearns to give me all the love I missed out on when I was growing up. He longs to fill me with so much of His caring, I am completely healed of the pain from my past.

When I let God have this place in my heart, He becomes my loving parent who always wants the very best for me. Then He can help me see myself as He sees me - precious, special, His priceless treasure who is close to His heart. As a result, I become less and less willing to accept what others have abusively told me I am.

This new identity empowers me to make sounder observations and wiser decisions about people. How God sees me and what He tells me, through His Word, becomes my new reference point for deciding which behaviors are acceptable in my interactions with others. Then, and only then, am I able to break the cycle of abuse in my life and establish healthy intimate relationships.

First, I explore the insights about "Papa God", because each of us needs a Dad!

* * *

"Papa God" wants to be my "Dad"!

A little girl needs to feel she is special to her father. She needs to feel that her Dad thinks she is pretty. In her heart of hearts, she wants to feel like she is his princess. A little boy needs his father to spend time with him. He needs his Dad to play ball with him, to come to his baseball games and share the things with him that are important to a little boy. He wants most of all, for his father to *be there* for him.

If my earthly father did not meet these needs, "Papa God" wants to adopt me. He wants to become that "Dad" I never had. I do not have to waste any more years of my life going from one destructive relationship after another, trying to fill that need. I can let "Papa God" have the place of a Dad in my heart and the healing process can move forward.

"You have not received a spirit of slavery leading to fear again,
but you have received a spirit of adoption,
by which you may cry out to Me, 'Abba Father'."
(Romans 8:15 NAS)
Personalized

(In the Greek, "Abba Father" is as personal and intimate a name for God as if I was saying to Him: "Papa God" or "dear Daddy".)

"See how very much I love you as a father.
I allow you to be called My child, and you really are."
(I John 3:1 NLT)
Personalized

"You are My very own child, adopted into My family,
calling Me 'Father, dear Father'."
(Romans 8:15 NLT)
Personalized

"Because you have become My child,
I sent the Spirit of My Son into your heart,
and now you can call Me, 'my dear Father'."
(Galatians 4:6 NLT)
Personalized

"You shall call Me, 'My Father'."
(Jeremiah 3:19 NAS)

"My unchanging plan has always been to adopt you into My own
family by bringing you to Myself through My Son, Jesus!"
(Ephesians 1:5 NLT)
Personalized

"If your father has abandoned you,
I, the Lord, want to adopt you.
I want to take care of you and hold you close."
(Psalms 27:10 NAS/Moffatt)
Personalized

"I sent My Son to buy your freedom
so that I could adopt you as My very own child."
(Galatians 4:5 NLT)
Personalized

"I want to be a father to you, if you've never had a father,
because I am a father to the fatherless."
(Psalm 68:5-6 NAS)
Personalized

"I would love to treat you as My own child...
I look forward to you calling Me 'Father'."
(Jeremiah 3:19 NLT)
Personalized

"Papa God" wants to "be there for me".

If I had an earthly father who was never there for me, I missed out on him sharing with me those special moments that any young child wants to share with his Dad.

I felt that way as a child.

Only the love from "Papa God" could heal the sadness that lingered in my heart. As soon as I fully grasped that I am His daughter, He began to make it up to me for what I missed out on with my earthly father. The dark cloud of rejection from that relationship left me. It did not return!

Contrary to what I experienced as a child, there is no disappointment in this love from "Papa God". He never lets me down. He is always "there for me", whenever I need a father's love.

"I will never fail you."
(Hebrews 13:5 NLT)

"Look behind you and I am there. Then look up ahead and I am there,
too. My reassuring Presence is with you, coming and going!"
(Psalm 139 The Message)
Personalized

"Place your trust in Me and you will not be disappointed."
(I Peter 2:6 NIV/NAS)
Personalized

"I am a trustworthy anchor for your soul.
I give you a hope that is both sure and steadfast."
(Hebrews 6:19 NLT/NAS)
Personalized

"Be assured. I am always with you."
(Psalm 16:8 NLT)
Personalized

"Papa God" feels the same way about me, as any loving Father feels about his child.

My "Papa God" is not a remote parent, who lives somewhere in the distant heavenlies. He is not a Father who is oblivious to what I am going through. He is the Creator of all. Yet, He is also my very own "Dad". He has the same concern for my welfare that any loving father has towards his child. He cares about me, just like the father in the following true story.

A catastrophic earthquake hit a small town in Russia. The shattered walls of a grammar school collapsed. A young boy and all his classmates were buried under a mountain of splintered wood and glass. The people in the town scrambled to reach the children, including the father of a young boy.

After fourteen hours, the people with the heavy equipment gave up. They left the site of the demolished school. The father kept digging. He was determined to find his son alive.

As the hours passed, one by one the people abandoned their rescue efforts and walked away. The father never gave up. Although all others had long gone, he kept searching for his son.

During all this time, the boy confidently reassured the other frightened children. "Don't worry," he told them. "I know my Dad. He won't give up until he finds me. You will all be safe, you'll see!"

Thirty-three hours after the violent earthquake shook this small Russian town, that father was still digging and searching, without stopping. In the thirty-fifth hour, he found his son and brought him to safety, along with all the children who were with him.

"See, I told you", the young boy said to his classmates, as they climbed out of the rubble that was once their schoolhouse. "I told you my Dad would come. I told you he wouldn't give up until he found me."

"Papa God" wants me to have the same, unwavering confidence in His love for me as the young Russian boy had in his father. He wants me to be able to say to myself, with absolute assurance, in all situations,

"My 'Papa God' cares about me just like a real Dad. He will find a way to help me, no matter what. He will never abandon His efforts to rescue me and help me!"

God's Word assures me that is exactly how He loves me!

"As a parent feels for his child, I feel for you."
(Psalm 103 The Message)
Personalized

"I have cared for you, again and again, in your time of wilderness, just as a father cares for his child."
(Deuteronomy 1:31 NLT)
Personalized

"I'll stick by you when you are down."
(Psalm 18 The Message)
Personalized

"When you cry out, 'I am slipping!'
My unfailing love will support you."
(Psalm 94:18 NLT)
Personalized

"If you'll hold on to Me for dear life, I'll get you out of any trouble.
I'll give you the best of care, if you'll only get to know and trust Me.
Call Me and I'll answer you. I'll be at your side in bad times.
I'll rescue you."
(Psalm 91 The Message)
Personalized

"You will not be shaken because I am right by your side."
(Psalm 16:8 NLT)
Personalized

"Papa God" gives me a sense of destiny and purpose,
just like any loving Father does for his child.

A father is meant to be a guiding influence in the life of his child. His encouragement and affirmation birth a sense of destiny in a child's young, impressionable heart. They build a confidence in that child that he has what it takes to succeed in life. Without that fatherly encouragement and support, I can wander aimlessly through life, robbed of any meaningful direction or goals.

If I didn't have a Dad, who communicated that he believed in me, "Papa God" wants to speak into my heart the words I need to hear a Father saying to me.

He fully understands that, without a purpose, hope dies on the inside of me. Therefore, He wants to tell me that He believes in me. He wants to speak into my life that He has complete confidence in His unique plan for my life.

He not only wants to encourage me in that plan, He has the power to help me fulfill it, because my destiny comes from Him!

"Without My vision for your life, you will perish."
(Proverbs 29:18 KJV)
Personalized

"I know the plans I have for you, plans to prosper you and not to harm you, plans to give you hope and a future."
(Jeremiah 29:11 NIV)
Personalized

"Be glad for all I am planning for you!"
(Romans 12:12 NLT)
Personalized

"I will work out My plans for your life."
(Psalm 138:8 NLT)
Personalized

*"I will keep on guiding you with My counsel.
I will lead you to a glorious destiny!"*
(Psalm 73:23-24 NLT)
Personalized

"Papa God" wants to hold me by the hand.

There is nothing more reassuring to a young child than walking by his father's side, with his little hand in his father's big, strong hand.

I never experienced that kind of assurance from the presence of my earthly father. I remember the day when I wished I could.

"Would you like to go to the park with me today?" Pop asked my older sister and me, early one morning.

"Sure, Pop," we told him, excitedly. With happy anticipation, we walked by his side to the bus stop.

Soon we boarded the bus that took us far from our home to a place I had never been. Finally, the ride ended. The door swung open and we stepped down to the curb.

"I have to go somewhere for just a few minutes," Pop told us, as soon as we arrived. "I promise, I'll be right back."

I watched, heavyhearted, as my father walked away from us down the street.

"He promised he'd come back soon," I comforted myself, over and over.

I sat on the grass, still wet with the early morning dew and waited for Pop to return. My sister wandered off to play by herself. Several hours went by. I continued to wait.

Not far from where I was sitting, a young girl and her father came into view. She walked by her father's side along a meandering pathway that was shrouded in trees. She had one of her hands securely in her father's big, strong hand. As I watched them, the father picked his daughter up and held her close on his shoulder.

"I wish I had a Dad like that," I said wistfully to myself. "I wish Pop was here and he would hold me like that so that I could feel safe and not hurt anymore."

After awhile, I grew weary of waiting. I walked around the park by myself, unable to enjoy being there. I kept hoping, at any moment, to see my father coming towards me.

Nighttime came. I was hungry and cold. For a long time, I watched a group of children having a birthday party at a large picnic area nearby. As soon as they left, I rummaged through the garbage pail by their table for leftover food.

Much later, Pop arrived.

"Sorry I took so long," he mumbled, apologetically.

"Where were you, Pop?" I asked him, trying to hold back my tears. "I waited so long for you!"

"I got tied up," was all he replied, while we walked, quickly, towards the bus.

I sat in silence next to Pop all the way home. I cried, quietly, as I stared out into the darkness of the night.

Now I have a "Papa God" who holds me by the hand, always just like that father did for his little girl in the park. My longing for the happiness I saw in the face of that little girl is fulfilled Whenever I remind myself that my hand is in the hand of my "Papa God", I feel secure. Most comforting of all, He never lets go of my hand, even if I mistakenly let go of His!

"Father, You've got my feet on the life path
that is all radiant from the shining of Your face.
Ever since You took my hand, I'm on the right way!"
(Psalm 16 The Message)
Personalized

"I will hold you by the hand and watch over you."
(Isaiah 42:6 NAS)
Personalized

"I am the Lord, your God,
who takes hold of your right hand and says to you,
'Do not be afraid. I will help you'."
(Isaiah 41:13 NAS)
Personalized

"When you fall, you will not be hurled headlong,
for I am the one who is holding you by the hand."
(Psalm 37:24 NAS)
Personalized

"Papa God" picks me up to carry me, when life gets too hard for me.

When life gets too "tough" for a young child, he needs to have his earthly father pick him up and carry him, just like the little girl in the park. This caring intervention from a loving father allows a child to relax inside. It gives him the confidence that he can "make it".

If I grew up without the arms of a father to pick me up and hold me when I felt overwhelmed, I can spend the rest of my life looking for someone to be that father to me that I never had. As a result, I establish relationships with people whom I think can take care of me and rescue me when life gets too hard. The problem is once I grow up no one can meet this need except "Papa God". He is the only one who can scoop me up into His Arms, no matter how old I get, whenever I need a Dad! Any efforts to fill that void, apart from His Father love, only ends in one disappointing relationship after another.

"Papa God" longs to intervene in my life and give me His Fatherly kindness and concern! He wants, even more than I do, to pick me up and hold me close to His heart, when life is too difficult for me to face.

"I lifted you and carried you through all the years."
(Isaiah 63:9 NLT)
·Personalized

"I carried you the way a father carries
his own son or daughter."
(Deuteronomy 1:31 NAS)
Personalized

"Each day I carry you in My arms."
(Psalm 68:19 NLT)
Personalized

"I will carry you in My arms and
hold you close to My heart."
(Isaiah 40:11 NLT)
Personalized

"Papa God" wants me to feel safe.

My father did not protect me from harm. It was not important to him that I felt safe. An incident that occurred when I was in late grammar school illustrates why I felt this way.

I slept in a room with red cement floors that had been converted from a kitchen into a small bedroom. The door to my room opened up into the front porch.

Late one night, I heard footsteps of someone running towards the porch. The steps came closer and closer. A fist smashed a glass panel. As the glass shattered, a man's gloved hand groped through the opening. I watched, in horror, as his fingers fumbled for the lock. At first, I was too frightened to make a sound. I wanted to scream. Instead, I froze, terrified.

"In another moment," I told myself, petrified. "He's going to be in my room."

"Help! Help!" I finally yelled out in a piercing scream.

My family rushed into the room. The man ran away and disappeared into the darkness outside.

"What's going on?" Pop mumbled, sleepily, from his bedroom. They shouted to him what had happened. He never came to make sure I felt safe.

After everyone left, I wondered if that man would come back to hurt me. Long after my family returned to their beds, I lay trembling under my blankets, too afraid to move. That was the night the dreams began of a man coming back to attack me.

After that traumatic night, fear took control of my life. Not until I had a revelation of "Papa God" as my Dad, twenty-one years later, did fear end its rule in my thoughts.

Through His Word, He taught me that I can run to Him, whenever I am afraid. His protective Presence can calm my worst fears. His Father love is bigger and stronger than any anxiety that can attack my mind. In His strong, reassuring arms, I can hide, whenever I am frightened. He shelters me, there, from any evil that comes against me. He even protects me as I sleep so that I can feel completely safe.

As a result of this understanding of "Papa God", a stability came into my emotions. An abiding peace calmed my spirit. The nightmares stopped! I was no longer a scared little girl inside. Instead, I became a secure, sheltered daughter of my "Papa God".

He extends that same fatherly protection to each of His children. Through His "Papa God" love, He wants each one to be delivered from the torment of his fears. Just like a real "Dad", it is of the utmost importance to Him that each one feels safe.

> *"Do not be afraid or discouraged, for I go before you.*
> *I am with you and I will not fail you."*
> *(Deuteronomy 31:8 NLT)*
> *Personalized*

> *"I am your refuge. My everlasting arms are under you."*
> *(Deuteronomy 33:27 NLT)*
> *Personalized*

> *"I am your strong fortress. I make your way safe."*
> *(II Samuel 22:33 NLT)*
> *Personalized*

> *"I am your hiding place. I protect you from trouble.*
> *I surround you with songs of victory!"*
> *(Psalm 32:7 NLT)*
> *Personalized*

> *"If you make Me your refuge, if you make Me your shelter,*
> *no evil will conquer you."*
> *(Psalm 91:9-10 NLT)*
> *Personalized*

> *"I surround you with a shield of love."*
> *(Psalm 5:12 NLT)*
> *Personalized*

> *"When you lie down, be at peace and sleep.*
> *I will keep you safe."*
> *(Psalm 4:8 NLT)*
> *Personalized*

"While I watch over you, I never get tired.
I never go to sleep!"
(Psalm 121:3-4 NLT)
Personalized

"I will keep a protective eye on you so that
you may dwell with Me in safety."
(Psalm 101:6 NLT)
Personalized

"You will pass safely through your sea of distress because
I will hold back the waves of the sea."
(Zechariah 10:11 NLT)
Personalized

"I, the Lord, am your Keeper and you are My vineyard.
I water you every moment, lest anyone damage you.
I guard you night and day. You can rely on My protection."
(Isaiah 27:3,5 NAS)
Personalized

"I alone am your refuge. I am your place of safety."
(Psalm 91:2 NLT)
Personalized

"Papa God" will never abandon me.

If my earthly father abandoned me, I didn't have a chance to know him at all. That rejection leaves a devastating scar that makes it difficult for me to establish healthy relationships as an adult. I perceive rejection, when it isn't really intended. I invite rejection, because I expect it to happen to me.

"Papa God" can restore all that I lost by not being wanted by my earthly father. He is a Father who really means it when He tells me He will never turn his back on me and walk out of my life, like my earthly father did. He is a faithful, caring Father, who keeps His promise to me that He will never, ever reject me!

"Do not be afraid or discouraged, for I go before you.
I am with you wherever you go."
(Joshua 1:9 NLT)
Personalized

"I have chosen you to be My own special treasure."
(Deuteronomy 14:2 NLT)
Personalized

"I will never desert you."
(Hebrews 13:5 NAS)

"I never abandon anyone who searches for Me."
(Psalm 9:10 NLT)
Personalized

"Even if your father abandons you, I will hold you close."
(Psalm 27:10 NLT)
Personalized

"When you go through deep waters and great trouble, I will be with you. "When you go through rivers of difficulty, you will not drown.
(Isaiah 43:2 NLT)

"Others may hit you when you are down, but I will stick by you."
(Psalm 18 The Message)
Personalized

"You can say to yourself, with confidence:
'My Father is my helper. I will not be afraid'."
(Hebrews 13:6 NAS)
Personalized

"Papa God" keeps His promises to me.

If I had an earthly father who did not keep his word to me, I learned I could not trust. To trust was to get my hopes up, only to be disappointed, over and over again.

I learned at a young age that I could not depend on my father to keep his promises to me. One incident, when I was eleven years old, is a vivid memory of his betrayal of my trust.

"Do you want to go with me to the movies?" Pop asked my older sister and me on a rainy Saturday afternoon.

"Oh, yes," we told him, excitedly.

"Will you stay with us, Pop?" I asked him, tentatively. I remembered the day he broke his promise to me and left me in the park until late at night.

"Oh yes, we'll have a great time together," he assured me. I smiled, happily, at the thought of spending time with Pop. I trusted him to keep his promise to me this time.

Moments later, we boarded a bus to take us to the movies.

The ride took much longer than I expected. We traveled to a theatre far from where we lived.

I didn't mind being so far from home because my father was with me.

Finally we arrived at the theatre and found seats close to the front. Pop sat down next to me. I smiled, contentedly, and snuggled close to him.

The lights went out. The movie, the House of Wax, flashed on the screen. Not long after it began, I realized that it was a scary movie. I never watched that type of movie because I was so easily frightened.

I pulled away from Pop and stiffened in my seat. I gripped the sides with both of my hands. The dark sounds of the music filled me with dread. I gasped, as a man's face cracked into pieces. Underneath was a grotesque corpse.

I screamed and turned to bury my face in Pop's shoulder. He was gone.

I wanted to run out of the theatre and look for him, but I was too afraid to move. Instead, I covered my eyes and forced myself to stay in my seat.

"Pop, where did you go?" I said to myself, crushed with disappointment. "You promised, Pop, that you'd stay with me. You promised..."

The movie finally ended. I rushed up the aisle to search for my father. He was nowhere to be found. My sister and I waited and waited. I was hungry and tired. I wanted to go home, but we were too far away to even know how to get there and we had no money for the bus fare.

I pressed my forehead against the large, cold window inside the theatre entrance and stared anxiously at the cars whizzing by outside.

"Where are you, Pop?" I wondered to myself. "Please come back..."

Hours later, he returned.

"By the way," Pop said, guiltily. "I couldn't stay. I had something I had to go take care of..."

"But you promised..." I started to say. He kept walking towards the bus stop and merely motioned for me to be still and follow him.

We sat a long time on a bench, waiting for the bus to arrive. I wrapped my arms tightly around me, but I still shivered in the harsh, cold wind. Finally, we boarded the bus. I sat by the window and turned my face away from Pop. I was too hurt to even cry.

There were other times when Pop didn't keep his word to me. Each incident made it more and more difficult for me to trust him. The damage from these layers of betrayal remained until "Papa God" became my "Dad". He does not make a promise and then break it, like my father did. He never builds me up, only to let me down!

Ever since "Papa God" became my "Dad", I am able to say, with absolute confidence, "I know my Papa God. He won't ever let me down."

"I love you, dearly.
Just because your father broke his promises to you,
does that mean that I will break My promises to you?

Of course not!
Though everyone else in the world is a liar,
I will stay true to you."
(Romans 1:7, 3:3-4 NLT)
Personalized

"I do not tell you to ask Me for something
that I do not plan to give you."
(Isaiah 45:19 NLT)
Personalized

"If a child asks her father for bread,
he doesn't trick her with sawdust, does he?

If she asks him for fish, he doesn't scare her with a live snake, does he?
As bad as you are, you wouldn't do that to your child.

So do you think that I, Your Father,
who conceived you in love, will do that to you?"
(Matthew Chapter Seven The Message)
Personalized

"I will never lie to you, nor change my mind.
I am not a man, that I would change my mind."
(I Samuel 15:29 NAS)
Personalized

"I am a Father who cannot lie!"
(Titus 1:2 NLT)
Personalized

"Not one of my words to you will fail."
(Joshua 23:14 NAS)
Personalized

"Without wavering, you can hold on tight to the hope you have in Me,
for I am a Father who can be trusted to keep His promises!"
(Hebrews 10:23 NLT)
Personalized

"I will not let any of My promises to you fail!"
(Psalm 89:33 NLT)
Personalized

"I will not take back a single word I said to you!"
(Psalm 89:34 NLT)
Personalized

*"Take new courage, for you can hold on to
what I promise you with confidence."
(Hebrews 6:18 NLT)
Personalized*

"Papa God" is kind and never harsh.

If I had an earthly father who expected too much of me, I learned to be too hard on myself. If my Dad was quick to get on my "case" whenever I made a mistake or whenever I did not live up to his expectations, I grew up feeling like a failure. I either decided it is not worth trying or I went to the other extreme and constantly tried to excel. In that case, I could never completely relax inside because of all the pressure I put on myself to succeed. I was driven to do whatever it takes to earn my father's approval.

My twenty-eight year old daughter, Mary, shared with me a compelling example of how it feels to not be able to live up to a father's harsh expectations.

"From as early as I can remember," she explained, *"I felt defeated by my Dad expecting too much from me and then being cruel when I couldn't measure up to what he wanted.*

I remember when I was nine years old. I clutched my report card proudly in my hand all the way home from the last day of school. As our house came into view at the end of the street, I told myself, confidently,

'I can hardly wait to show Dad my grades. I know he'll be so proud of me for getting all 'A's and just one 'B'.'

The 'B' was in Math! I hated Math, but I worked my very best all year long to earn a good grade in it. I was especially proud of that 'B' because I worked so hard to get it.

'Look, Dad,' I said to him, excitedly, as soon as he walked through the front door later that afternoon. 'Look at my report card. I did real good! I know you'll be proud of me.'

Beaming with pride, I handed it to him. My smile quickly faded. I watched, anxiously, as he examined my report card with a serious expression on his face.

'What's this 'B' all about?' he finally said, disapprovingly. 'You could have done better than that in Math, if you had tried harder!'

'But I tried so hard in math, Dad. And the 'A's. Aren't you happy...' I didn't get to finish what I was saying, before he interrupted me.

'The 'B' isn't good enough!' he said, completely ignoring all of my 'A's. 'I expect an 'A' in math next time!'

My Dad acted like I hadn't accomplished anything at all. All he focused on was what he considered a negative.

I stared at him in disbelief. Without another word, he handed the report card back to me and walked away from me down the steps to the garage.

I ran to my bedroom, crushed by his disappointment in me. I threw myself, face down, on my bed and buried my sobs in the pillow.

'I'll just have to try harder,' I told myself, as a torrent of tears stung my cheeks. 'That's all I can do. Somehow, I'll have to try harder.'

I was too young to understand that my father's expectations were impossible to live up to. I simply blamed myself for not being good enough!

That scenario happened over and over, every time I brought a report card home from school.

By the time I got to Junior High, I had given up on school. I didn't care anymore. I knew that no matter how hard I tried to please my Dad, my efforts would never be good enough.

'So why bother trying,' I eventually concluded."

**Mary's decision to give up
is a sobering example of why God tells fathers:**

"Don't provoke your children!

*If you do, they will become discouraged
and quit trying."*
(Colossians 3:21 NAS/NLT)

"Papa God" is a very different kind of Father.

He is not a stern, harsh taskmaster. He is not watching me so that He can criticize me the minute I make a mistake. He is never cruel. He will never do anything to hurt me. He does not demand perfection of me. He will not crush me with discouraging expectations that I can never live up to.

Instead, He is a Dad who knows me inside and out. He genuinely understands me and my every weakness. He affirms me so that I can have the confidence to face the challenges of life. He encourages me so that I can feel good about myself. He accepts me for who I am!

When I "blow" it, He extends to me a father's compassion. He understands that I need His love the most, when I have failed.

"I made your heart,
so I understand everything you do."
(Psalm 33:15 NLT)
Personalized

"I understand how weak you are."
(Psalm 103:14 NLT)
Personalized

"I know you inside and out."
(Psalm 139 The Message)
Personalized

Others look at your outward appearance,
but I look at your heart."
(I Samuel 16:7 NAS)
Personalized

"I look deep within your mind and heart."
(Psalm 7:9 NLT)
Personalized

"I see your heart and I understand."
(I Chronicles 28:9 NLT)
Personalized

"I bend down and listen to you."
(Psalm 116:2 NLT)
Personalized

"Just as a father has compassion on his child,
I have compassion on you!"
(Psalm 103:13 NAS)
Personalized

"Papa God" corrects me, but only out of love!

If my earthly father abused me when he corrected me, I learned to fear his harsh discipline. I grew up equating being corrected with pain. I wanted to run away from him, when I "blew it". I never was able to experience that a caring father corrects his child with love, not out of anger, or a total disregard for his feelings.

My daughter's story illustrates the damage a father's harsh discipline inflicts on a child.

"I always felt, growing up," Mary explained to me, one morning, recently, "that my father's motivation for disciplining me was to control my opinions and feelings.

No matter what I talked to him about, he was always right and I was always wrong.

Just because I was a child or a teenager, what I had to say or how I felt was never valid to him. If I didn't completely and immediately agree with him, he grabbed me, hit me or said cruel words to me. He demanded my respect, but he never treated me with respect. He never tried to understand me.

'You are the child and I am the parent,' I remember him telling me, whenever I objected to him being mean or degrading towards me.

'God does not command me to respect you, but the Bible tells you to respect me,' he always insisted.

By the time I went into Junior High, I felt no one wanted to understand me. I turned my anger towards my father against anyone in authority who came down hard on me.

I rebelled, if I ever thought someone was making a judgment about me, without listening to my opinions or feelings. I had no respect for anyone who didn't treat me, also, with respect."

The suffering my daughter experienced is repeated in the life of any child whose father abuses his child through harsh discipline.

"Papa God" wants the best for me. That is the only reason He ever corrects me. He does not "beat me over the head" with His Word. His correction does not destroy me. It does not frighten me. His Presence in my life, as a "Dad", does not leave me feeling degraded or abused. He does not try to control me.

Instead, He encourages me to make the right choices myself so that He can bless my life. He warns me when I am going in the wrong direction, but only to protect me from doing the things that will end up hurting me. He only wants to help me have a happy life.

"Don't be discouraged when I correct you.
I only discipline those I love and those who accept Me as their Father!
As you endure My discipline, remember that
I am treating you as My very own child."
(Hebrews 12:5-7 NLT)
Personalized)

"My child, don't ignore it when I discipline you.
Don't be discouraged when I correct you.
I only correct those I love, just as a father corrects
his child in whom he delights."
(Proverbs 3:11-12 NLT)
Personalized

"My discipline is always right and
it is always what is good for you."
(Hebrews 12:10 NLT)
Personalized

"I discipline you only to help you."
(Deuteronomy 8:5 NLT)
Personalized

"Papa God" will never hurt me

My daughter shares her devastation from being emotionally and verbally abused by someone she trusted to not hurt her, *"because he is my Dad"*:

"When I was thirteen years old, I was arrested for stealing candy from the convenience store across the street from Junior High School. Mom had to pick me up at the police station.

I knew she was upset and I felt bad that I had hurt her, but Dad was the one I dreaded seeing. By this time, he already had a history of being verbally and physically abusive towards me. I was scared he would beat me up for this incident.

I sat tensely on the living room couch, waiting for Dad to come home from work. As soon as I heard his car in the driveway, I panicked.

'Look at what you've done now,' he screamed at me as he stormed into the room and stood angrily in front of me.

He towered over where I sat on the couch and glared at me. His face was contorted with the utter revulsion he felt towards me.

'I....'

Before I could finish, he spit on my face!

Instant rage welled up inside me. I wiped his spit off my face with my sleeve.

'You have no right to do that to me,' I yelled at him. 'You have no right!'

'You're a loser,' he screamed back at me. 'That's what you are, a loser! And I have every right to treat you any way I want. You got exactly what you deserve. God is just as disgusted with you as I am!'

He then quoted Scriptures that proved God supported him acting so cruelly towards me.

I ran out of the room and into my bedroom, as he shouted at me, 'You get back here right this minute! I'm not finished with you yet.'

I slammed the door behind me and slumped to the floor by my bed in tears.

I was relieved my Dad didn't come after me and force me to go back into the livingroom.

'I feel like scum under his feet,' I told myself, as my chest heaved with deep sobs. 'I'm nothing to my father but a piece of dirt!'

At that moment, I wished I could die. I would rather he had taken a knife and killed me, than live with how degraded I felt from his spit that I could still feel on my face.

From that day, I wanted to hurt my Dad as much as he had hurt me. I tried many times to kill myself. I remember saying to myself, often,

'If I have to hurt like this all of the time, what's the point of living?'"

As Mary grew older, she suffered from a crippling emotional pain that almost destroyed her.

She had witnessed her father's violence towards me as a young child. When I remarried, the cruelty from her second father crushed tender places inside of her. Anger and hatred consumed her.

Mary turned to drugs. She lived with different men. They used and mistreated her. Then they discarded her, as if she was a worthless piece of trash. Eventually, she lived on the streets of the town where she grew up, troubled, scared and lost.

No matter how much I wished it were possible, I could not change the past and erase all her pain. I could not undo all the damage. I could only pray that some day God would "make it up to her for the years the locusts had destroyed in her life" (Joel 2:25).

God often awakened me from sleep and warned me to pray for Mary's safety. Inevitably, days later, she appeared at my doorstep. Underneath the heavy makeup and hardened countenance, I saw a frightened little girl, who desperately needed to know that her family still loved her.

"You were praying for me the other night, Mom," she would say, with a haunted look in her eyes.

"I know you were praying for me. It's your prayers that protected me. I would have been killed, Mom, if you hadn't been praying."

Then, just as quickly as she had come, she walked away and disappeared down the street. I ached for her, but all I could do is trust God to protect her, until she found her way back to Him.

When Mary was twenty-six years old, God answered all my prayers! She became so scared by what was happening in her life that she chose to enter the Minnesota Teen Challenge. Their dedicated staff ministered to her for over a year. Through their love, their powerfully anointed teaching and personal ministry, my daughter returned to the Jesus she had been running away from since early high school. She was delivered from drugs and demonic spirits. She was set free from the deadly anguish in her soul.

The days of being consumed with angry hatred were over. Mary forgave her father. She forgave herself for all her choices that had caused her and the people she loves so much pain. She began a new life.

Mary served as a ministry intern for six months after she graduated from Teen Challenge. Then my restored daughter returned home! Our new friendship quickly washed away our regrets for all the years we had missed out on as mother and daughter.

Mary found a job and enrolled in college. She immediately excelled in both! Layer upon layer, God restored to her all the self-respect and family relationships that she had lost.

When a child grows up with the kind of abuse Mary experienced, the word "Father" or "Dad" becomes synonymous with pain.

As a result, it becomes extremely difficult for that child to want to have anything to do with God as his "Abba Father". Mike's troubling story further illustrates how a father's abuse can turn a son or daughter away from the Lord.

Mike was seventeen, when Dave, one of his best friends, was killed in a car accident. Dave was a straight "A" student. He was active in the youth group in his church. Even though he was only seventeen, he was a strong Christian. He was what Mike would call "a really good kid".

All of Mike's other friends were always ditching school, partying and getting "stoned". Jim was the only one who stayed out of trouble.

Then, one day, the phone call came telling Mike of Dave's tragic death.

Mike was shocked by what the voice on the other end of the line was telling him.

"He's dead, Mike! Dave's dead!"

Mike hung up the phone and sat, stunned, in a chair across from his Dad.

"Why Dave, Dad?" he said in a loud, hurt voice.

"Why did God let him die? He was such a good person...such a good Christian. Why did God let this happen?"

His father listened, in silence.

"If anybody deserved to die, it's all my other friends, the ones who are just "stoners", Mike continued, angry and confused.

"Screw God for doing this! Screw Him for letting Dave die!" Mike yelled.

Without any warning, his Dad leaped out of his chair and lunged at Mike. He was a tall, solidly built man. With all his strength, he slugged his son in the face.

"You don't talk about God like that!" he told Mike, indignantly.

At that moment, Mike needed compassion from his Dad, not a condemning, self-righteous rebuke. He needed his father to understand his overwhelming grief and confusion.

Mike shut down on God after that incident. He already had been struggling with how he felt about Christianity. His father's cruelty, in defense of God, caused him to shut Him out completely. He didn't want anything to do with the God his Dad believed in!

To all the Mikes and "Marys", who do not want to give God the Father a chance to be their Dad because of abuse they suffered from their earthly father, "Papa God" wants them to know...

"I do not enjoy hurting you or causing you sorrow."
(Lamentations 3:33 NLT)
Personalized

"I will rescue you and you will no longer be abused and destroyed."
(Ezekiel 34:22 NLT)
Personalized

"I show compassion to you according
to the greatness of my unfailing love for you."
(Lamentations 3:32 NLT)
Personalized

"Never feel like you have to hide your feelings from Me."
(Psalm 34 The Message)
Personalized

"Open up before Me and keep nothing back.
I'll do whatever needs to be done."
(Psalm 37 The Message)
Personalized

"I will never let you down.
I'll never look the other way, when you are being kicked around.
I will never wander off and do My own thing.
I'll be right here, listening to you."
(Psalm 22 The Message)
Personalized

"I am a safe house for the battered.
I am a sanctuary for you in your bad times.
The moment you arrive, you can relax.
You will never be sorry you knocked!"
(Psalm 9 The Message)
Personalized

"I will not crush you when you are weak.
I will not quench your smallest hope."
(Isaiah 42:3 NLT)
Personalized

"Papa God" wants to heal me.

If I had an earthly father who leaned on me for his emotional or sexual needs, the scars go deep. Troubled, confused feelings come into my young heart. The father I trusted to love me violated me. He betrayed me.

My brother's life is a tragic example of the damage from a father's sick dependency on a child for his adult needs.

Joe was born when I was eight. As soon as he came home from the hospital, he was left alone in his crib most of the time. I tried as hard as I could to give him the love he was missing, but I could never give him enough affection to make up for Mom and Pop's neglect.

As Joe got older, Pop developed an unhealthy bond with him. The more distant my father's relationship with Mom became, the more Pop leaned on Joe for his need for companionship. Joe was starved for love, just like Pop. The two grew increasingly more dependent on each other. Each day they spent hours alone together.

When Joe was in late grammar school, Pop's health deteriorated. He leaned more and more on Joe to be close to him. This was a heavy emotional burden for such a young boy.

Joe felt responsible to meet his father's needs. He did not go out to play. He didn't do any of the things a boy his age usually would do.

"Could you stay home with me," Pop asked Joe, early one morning, just before Joe walked out the door to go to school. "I don't want to be alone today. I really need you to be with me."

Joe struggled. He was visibly torn. He didn't want to miss out on what was happening at school that day, but he also didn't want to let Pop down.

"No, Pop," Joe finally said, guiltily. "I really want to go to school. My teacher is doing something special with us today. We're having a party."

With those words, my brother shrugged his shoulders and left for school.

Pop died not long after that. Joe never forgave himself for not staying home with his father. A relentless guilt battered him.

When Joe started high school, he escaped from his pain into drugs and heavy drinking. He failed all his classes. In a fit of rage, he attacked Mom. Shaken and alarmed, she called the police and they took Joe away.

By the time he was eighteen, my brother was in and out of mental hospitals. His violent, bizarre behaviors could only be controlled by potent drugs. He was subjected to numerous shock treatments that permanently stripped him of his original personality. I watched the brother I loved become someone I no longer knew. It was as if the real Joe had already died.

"I can't get over that I let Pop down," he explained to me, one day, when I visited him in a locked hospital ward. "I can't get it out of my mind that I left him when he needed me."

Joe never sat up straight enough to look me in the eye. His head hung low the entire time. His shoulders were stooped, as if bowed over under the weight of his guilt.

As much as I loved my brother and grieved over the tragic direction of his life, I could not help him. He became more and more dangerous to be around. As he grew older, he spent more of his days locked up in psychiatric facilities. Joe never came back to the person he was before Pop died.

If my father violated me - if he used me to meet his sexual or emotional needs, I may not end up as disturbed as my brother, Joe. Nonetheless, the scars leave me damaged in vulnerable places in my soul.

No human effort can remove this damage. I cannot heal my own scars, but I have an "Abba Father" who can! He understands my shame and guilt. Because He understands exactly how much I am suffering, He wants to take all the troubled feelings out of me and give me a new heart. He not only wants to do all this for me, He is the only one who can!

In Chapter Seven, I share about a breakdown that I experienced the year after I was saved. If "Papa God" had not become my Father, I have no doubt I would have ended up as sick as my brother Joe. That breakdown could have destroyed me.

God's Father love can be that vital to someone who has been abused and violated by his earthly Dad. For that reason, "Papa God" offers this love to each of His children who need Him to heal the wounds from their past.

"Cry out to Me and I will heal you."
(Psalm 30:2 NLT)
Personalized

"I will bind up your fractures and heal your bruises."
(Isaiah 30:26 NAS)
Personalized

"I will rebuild the ruined places in your life."
(Ezekiel 36:36 NAS)
Personalized

"I will restore you to health and heal your wounds."
(Jeremiah 30:17 NAS)
Personalized

"I will give you a new heart."
(Ezekiel 36:26 NAS)
Personalized

"I will set your heart free."
(Psalms 119:32 NIV)
Personalized

"I will put your life back together."
(Psalms 18 and 19 The Message)
Personalized

"I will make your life complete,
if you place all the pieces before Me.
I will give you a fresh start!
I will rewrite the text of your life,
when you open the book of your heart to My eyes!"
(Psalm 18 The Message)
Personalized

"I will pull you up out of the grave
and give you another chance at life!"
(Psalm 30 The Message)
Personalized

"Only throw open the doors of your heart to Me.
Then you will discover, at that very moment,
that I have thrown open My door to you.
You will find yourself standing
where you always hoped you might stand,
out in the wide-open spaces of My grace and glory,
standing tall and shouting your praise!"
(Romans Chapter Five The Message)
Personalized

Chapter Six

ℐ need a "ℳom"!

I grew up in a home where there was no love, no comfort, no tender moments of closeness to my mother. If the Holy Spirit had not become, in every sense of the words, my comforter and the provider of nurturing to me, I would not be a whole person today. That part of me that only a mother can touch, would never have been restored.

The insights in this chapter into the "mother love" of the Holy Spirit are seldom taught, yet they were profoundly instrumental in transforming my life. For that reason, each one is a priceless treasure...

> *"I rejoice in Your Word*
> *like one who finds a great treasure!"*
> *(Psalm 119:162 NLT)*

If you are hurting because your mother could not love you as a child, it is my earnest hope that these powerful insights will restore the broken places deep on the inside of you.

May they help you, also, to receive from the Holy Spirit that same comforting, nurturing love.

* * *

*The primary role of the Holy Spirit
in my life is to be my Comforter.*

*"I will ask the Father, and He will give you another Comforter
who will never leave you. He is the Holy Spirit.
I will not abandon you as orphans.
The comforter will come, whom I will send to you
from the Father. He will tell you all about Me."
(John 14:16,18-15:26 Amplified/NLT)
Personalized*

*"I, even I, am the one who comforts you."
(Isaiah 51:12 NLT)*

*To be a comforter is also the primary role
that a mother has in the life of her child.*

*"I will comfort you ...
as a child is comforted by its mother."
(Isaiah 66:13 NLT)*

*The following are the many ways that the
Holy Spirit can fulfill this need for a
mother's comfort and nurturing.*

* * *

*The Holy Spirit has loved me,
the same way a mother does,
ever since I was in my mother's womb.*

As a child, the cry of my heart was, "Won't someone please love me!" The older I got, the more intensely I felt, "I have never really been wanted, not even when Mom was pregnant with me." These feelings of rejection poisoned every aspect of my life. They drove me to try to find someone to fulfill my longing to feel loved, but that hunger could not be satisfied.

Then one day, the Holy Spirit revealed to me that He has loved me, even from my mother's womb. Before I ever hurt with my first feeling of rejection from my earthly mother, He was there, wanting me to be His child.

These are the words the Holy Spirit ministered to me to help me understand this truth. They are for every person who needs a Mom:

"Even when your mother was pregnant with you, I was there watching you, loving you, caring about you. I was so excited about when you would be born, I already had wonderful plans for you. Yes! You are a wanted child. You are not a mistake. You are so important to me, I planned for you to have the gift of life before you were even conceived in your mother's womb. Precious child of mine, if your own mother has rejected you, I want you and I always have. You are that precious to me. You are my treasure that I always hold close to my heart."

God's Word confirms that the Holy Spirit loves me in exactly this way!

"I speak to you deep in your heart to tell you, 'You are My child'."
(Romans 8:16 NLT)
Personalized

"When you were born, no one cared about you.
No one had the slightest interest in you.
No one pitied you or cared for you.
On the day you were born, you were left to die, unwanted.
But I came by and saw you there, helplessly kicking about...
As you lay there, I said, 'Live!'
And I helped you to thrive like a plant in the field.
You grew up and became a beautiful jewel."
(Ezekiel 16:4-7 NLT)

"I have cared for you since before you were born.
I have chosen you and I will not reject you.
I'll not throw you away."
(Isaiah 46:3, 41:9 NAS/NLT)
Personalized

"Even if your mother abandons you, I will hold you close."
(Psalm 27:10 NLT)
Personalized

"I will hold you close to my heart."
(Isaiah 40:11 NLT)
Personalized

"I will not reject you.
I will not abandon you, My own special possession."
(Psalm 94:14 NLT)
Personalized

"I have chosen you for Myself, for My own special treasure."
(Psalm 135:4 NLT)
Personalized

"You are precious when I look at you and I love you."
(Isaiah 43:4 NAS)
Personalized

"Can a mother forget her nursing child?
Can she feel no love for a child she has borne?
But even if that were possible, I would not forget you.
See, I have written your name on My hand."
(Isaiah 49:15-16 NLT)

"You will be nursed at My breasts,
carried in My arms and treated with love.
I will comfort you there as a child
is comforted by its mother."
(Isaiah 66:12-13 Amplified/NLT)
Personalized

"I made all the delicate, inner parts of your body
and knit you together in your mother's womb.
I watched you as you were being formed in utter seclusion,
as you were being woven together in the dark of the womb.
I saw you before you were born.
Every day of your life was recorded in My book.
Every moment was laid out before a single day had passed."
(Psalm 139:13, 15-16 NLT)
Personalized

"I have been with you from birth.
From your mother's womb I have cared for you."
(Psalm 71:6 NLT)
Personalized

The Holy Spirit knows me intimately.

A loving Mom has an intimate relationship with her child. She is aware of him, even when he is at a distance. She understands how her child is feeling, including many of those things that he does not speak.

The Holy Spirit also knows me intimately. He knows the number of hairs on my head. He understands my every thought and feeling. He watches me and is continually aware of where I am. He even knows what I am going to say, before I speak it.

> *"You are an open book to me.*
> *Even from a distance, I know what you are thinking.*
> *I know when you leave and when you get back.*
> *You are never out of My sight.*
>
> *I know everything you are going to say, before you start the first*
> *sentence...I know you inside and out."*
> *(Psalm 139 The Message)*
> *Personalized*

> *"I have examined your heart. I know everything about you.*
> *I know when you sit down and when you stand up.*
> *I know your every thought when you are far away...*
> *Every moment, I know where you are."*
> *(Psalm 139:1-3 NLT)*
> *Personalized*

> *"I pay great attention to you, down to the last detail.*
> *I have even numbered the hairs on your head."*
> *(Matthew Chapter Ten The Message)*
> *Personalized*

The Holy Spirit knows me by my own name.

I am not lost to the Holy Spirit among the vast sea of faces that make up all the people in the world. I am not a nameless grain of sand among the millions of grains of sand on the seashore of life. Quite the contrary! God knows me personally, by my own name.

It's a beautiful name. He gave it to me while I was still in my mother's womb.

"I called you by name when you did not know Me."
(Isaiah 45:4 NLT)

"From within the womb, I called you by name.
(Isaiah 49:1 NLT)
Personalized

"I have called you by name. You are Mine."
(Isaiah 43:1 NLT)

The Holy Spirit sings over me.

When my children were little, I tucked them into bed and sang to them, until they fell asleep. One day the Holy Spirit showed me that He sings over me, just like I did for my children. Through His songs, He calms me with His love, as a mother calms her young child.

"I will rejoice over you with great gladness.
I will take great delight in you.
With My love, I will calm all your fears.
I will quiet you with My love.

I will exult over you by singing a happy song.
I will rejoice over you with singing."
(Zephaniah 3:17 NLT/KJV)
Personalized

The Holy Spirit responds to my needs with tenderness.

As a child, I often sat alone on the top step of our old wooden porch. I wrapped my arms around my knees and hugged them, tightly, to my chest.

"I wish Mom would come and spend time with me today." I told myself. "Just this once..."

"I'm too busy", she typically replied, when I asked her.

I waited and hoped, many a day, but Mom never came.

The Holy Spirit now fills this need in my life for a mother who wants to be with me. He always has time for me. In fact, He absolutely loves it when I come into His Presence to spend time with Him. He looks forward to every special moment He can be close to me. When I call out to Him, as I once did to Mom from that porch, He listens. He responds, immediately, to any cry of my heart. My needs are of the utmost importance to Him. He fully understands these needs, even better than I do myself.

"I care about what happens to you."
(I Peter 5:7 NLT)
Personalized

"I care what happens to you, even more than you do."
(Matthew Chapter Ten The Message)
Personalized

"I care enough to respond to you when you seek Me."
(Hebrews Chapter Eleven The Message)
Personalized

*"I know the hopes of the helpless.
I will surely listen to your cries and comfort you."*
(Psalm 10:17 NLT)
Personalized

"I will respond, instantly, to the sound of your cries."
(Isaiah 30:19 NLT)
Personalized

*"I respond to you as surely as the arrival of dawn
or the coming of rains in early spring."*
(Hosea 6:3 NLT)
Personalized

"With a love that never ends, I have compassion on you."
(Isaiah 54:8 NLT)
Personalized

"I caress you with My gentle ways."
(Psalm 18 The Message)
Personalized

The Holy Spirit wipes away my tears.

I cried myself to sleep many a night, growing up. They were always private tears. Mom never held me or comforted me. She never wiped away my tears.

All that unhappiness is behind me now!

I never have to cry alone again! The Holy Spirit's love is so tender towards me, He even wants to dry my tears.

"I keep track of all your sorrows.
I have collected all your tears in My bottle.
I have recorded each one in My book."
(Psalm 56:8 NLT)
Personalized

"I will wipe away all your tears."
(Isaiah 25:8 NLT)
Personalized

The Holy Spirit accepts me as I am. I am not a mistake!

I grew up feeling like a mistake.

I watched, from a distance, everyone around me at school, as they laughed and talked and had fun. I never felt a part of what they were doing. I didn't fit anywhere. I didn't belong to anyone. The loneliness of living on the outside, looking in, followed me everywhere I went.

I felt especially lonely whenever I thought about Mom.

I wanted to share my accomplishments with her. I remember the times I worked hard on my part in a school play or a Christmas program. I dreamed of Mom coming to see me perform. I wanted to know she was watching me and sharing my world with me. I wanted her to be proud of me. Yet, whenever I looked out over the sea of faces, at all the other parents, Mom was never there. My hopes always ended in crushing disappointment.

Years later, the Holy Spirit reached into my heart and gave me His full acceptance. From that moment, I was no longer an outsider, looking in. I no longer felt like a mistake!

I finally belonged to someone who made me feel wanted and special. I put my disappointment about Mom behind me. I embraced, completely, the nurturing that the Holy Spirit poured into my heart. I became His exceedingly loved child and I knew He was proud to call me His daughter.

"I have made you accepted in Me, the Beloved."
(Ephesians 1:6 KJV)
Personalized

"You now have the free gift of being accepted by Me!"
(Romans 5:16 NLT)
Personalized

"I call nobodies and make them somebodies.
I call the unloved and make them beloved.
In the place where they yelled out, 'You're nobody!'
They're calling you 'My living child'.
(Romans Chapter Nine The Message)
Personalized

"I will validate your life in the clear light of day.
I'll stamp you with approval at high noon."
(Psalm 37 The Message)
Personalized

The Holy Spirit hurts every time I hurt,

just as a mother hurts for her child.

A loving Mom cares deeply, when she sees that her child is troubled. Nothing causes her greater heartache than to know her child is hurting. The Holy Spirit has always cared about me, in that same way.

Whenever I was sad, as a little girl, because I didn't have a Mom who loved me, the Holy Spirit saw what was happening to me.

He grieved every time I hurt. He wept over my life, just as Jesus wept over Jerusalem. Every time I was abused and rejected, He wanted to reach down and help me. He longed to scoop me up into His arms to shelter me, just as a mother hen protectively gathers her chick under her wings, but He couldn't.

The Holy Spirit had to wait until I could look up and see Him offering me His comfort and nurturing. He had to wait until I understood how much He wanted to help me. He had to wait until I was willing to receive that help. Only then could He pour his healing love into my broken heart.

"As a parent feels for her child, I feel for you."
(Psalm 103 The Message)
Personalized

"I have seen your troubles, and I care about the anguish of your soul."
(Psalm 31:7 NLT)
Personalized

"My child, My child, how often I wanted to gather you to Me
the way a hen gathers her chicks under her wings,
but you were unwilling."
(Matthew 23:37 NAS)
Personalized

"I have never let you down.
I have never looked the other way
when you were being kicked around.
I have never wandered off to do My own thing.
I have been right there, listening."
(Psalm 22 The Message)
Personalized

"In all your suffering, I suffered."
(Isaiah 63:9 NLT)
Personalized

The Holy Spirit gives me a place to come back home to.

"Lord, through all generations, You have been our home."
(Psalm 90:1 NLT)

No matter how old they grow, a mother cannot rest until she knows that each of her children is doing well. To her dying breath, her overriding desire is that each one finds a happy, full life.

Although she feels all this concern, a mother, who has a healthy love for her children, will not do for them what they need to do for themselves. She does not encourage a dependency on her that hinders a son or daughter from making a successful transition into adult independence. However, if one of them needs help, and it's in her child's best interest for her to provide it, she will sacrifice whatever she must in order to extend her help.

At times, this help is a physical home to come back to when a young adult needs a safe, supportive place to stay, temporarily, as he reestablishes his life.

At other times of crisis or crushing brokenness, that home is not necessarily a physical place. It is a place a person can come back to in his heart where he knows no matter what his Mom loves him. She cares about what happens to him. She wants the best for him. Her love is a home away from home, a safe haven for his battered soul.

This normal concern of a mother for her older children was missing in my mother. Once my father died, life improved drastically for Mom. Her depression left. She remarried and had a new life with ample finances. She had a lovely home, new friends and took pride in her appearance. Even though life got easier for Mom, she had none of the feelings towards her children that are a natural part of being a mother.

The older I got, the more I was convinced that if I was drowning, and Mom had the only lifeline to throw to me to get me to a place of safety, she wouldn't throw it. She would walk away from me and let me drown.

Consequently, after I left home at eighteen, I only asked her for help two times. I turned to her for a physical place of refuge, when I left the convent. She pushed me away. I then floundered in a turbulent sea of disastrous choices. Seven years later, I was in an even more desperate situation. Her love being a home I could come back home to for emotional support could have radically changed the direction of my life.

I had just ended a physically abusive marriage. Shaken and scared, I was not coping well with the trauma from my husband's recent violence.

"Mom, he tried to kill me," I told her on the phone, my voice trembling. "I was so scared. But I've left him, Mom. I finally know that's what I need to do."

She listened, in silence.

"I have no one to turn to," I explained further, unable to hide the panic I was feeling. "I have no friends. I was always so ashamed of the abuse; I didn't let anyone get close to me. I..."

"I can't help you", she said, abruptly, before I could finish my sentence. "You'll have to work it out for yourself."

After an awkward silence, I ended the conversation. My mother's coldness only added to the frightening uncertainty that gripped me.

Years later, the Holy Spirit showed me in His Word that I never again had to feel that devastating abandonment. He gave me a place in His love where I always have a refuge from the storms of life.

I now live every moment in the reality of this sheltering love. As a result, Mom's rejection has no power over me anymore.

Now and forever, I have a place to come back home to in the Holy Spirit! In that home, I will always receive a warm welcome and all the support I could ever need!

*"I have been your home forever,
long before the mountains were born,
long before I birthed the earth itself."
(Psalm 90 The Message)
Personalized*

*"I am the one who looks after you and cares for you."
(Hosea 14:8 NLT)*

*"I will support you."
(Isaiah 42:6 NLT)
Personalized*

*I will be a sanctuary for you.
(Isaiah 8:14 NAS)
Personalized*

*"I do not ignore your suffering.
I do not turn and walk away.
I listen to your cries for help."
(Psalm 22:24 NLT)
Personalized*

"I am concerned for you and I will come to help you."
(Ezekiel 36:9 NLT)

"I enjoy helping you."
(Psalm 35:27 NLT)
Personalized

"I will shield you with My wings and shelter you with My feathers.
If you make your shelter in Me,
no evil will conquer you!"
(Psalm 91:4, 9-10 NLT)
Personalized

"I am a shelter for you from the storm and the wind."
(Isaiah 32:2 NLT)
Personalized

"I am a refuge from the storms of life.
If you are in need and in distress,
I am a shelter for you from the rain..."
(Isaiah 25:4 NLT)
Personalized

"Hide beneath the shadow of my wings
until this violent storm is past."
(Psalm 57:1 NLT)
Personalized

"Come home to Me, again, for I am merciful."
(Jeremiah 3:12 NLT)

"Make your home in Me just as I do in you...
Make yourself at home with Me..."
(John Chapter Fifteen The Message)

"I make a home for you when you are lonely.
I bring you home."
(Psalm 68:6 NAS/Moffatt)
Personalized

"I will bring you home again...
You will return and will have peace and quiet
and nothing will make you afraid."
(Jeremiah 46:27 NLT)
Personalized

"I will be a welcoming refuge to you."
(Joel 3:16 NLT)
Personalized

"I will make a pathway in your wilderness
for you to come home."
(Isaiah 43:19 NLT)
Personalized

"Tears of joy will stream down your face
and I will lead you home with great care."
(Jeremiah 31:9 NLT)
Personalized

"You will come home and sing songs of joy...
You will be radiant because of the many
gifts I will give you...
Your life will be like a watered garden and
all your sorrows will be gone."
(Jeremiah 31:12 NLT)
Personalized

The Holy Spirit will never change how He feels about me.

This comforting, nurturing, healing love from the Holy Spirit is mine forever. It does not change. It does not come and go. I can depend on this love every moment of every day of my life.

With unfailing love I have drawn you to myself."
(Jeremiah 31:3 NLT)
Personalized

"Though the mountains be shaken and the hills be removed,
My unfailing love for you will never be shaken.
My promise of peace will never be removed from you,
because I have compassion on you."
(Isaiah 54:10 NIV/NAS)
Personalized

"I will never stop loving you."
(Psalm 89:33 NLT)
Personalized

The Holy Spirit will love me like a "Mom" does, no matter how old I get.

No matter how old I am, I still need to know that I have a mother who loves me. If a mother's love has always been missing, the pain of that loss hurts even more deeply as I get older.

The Holy Spirit understands this need. He reassures me that my face may wrinkle. My hair may turn white with age. However, to Him, I am always just His child. He always loves me, just like a "Mom".

> *"I will be your God throughout your lifetime-*
> *until your hair is white with age.*
> *I made you, and I will care for you."*
> *(Isaiah 46:3-4 NLT)*

The Holy Spirit wants to make it up to me for all the lost years.

The Holy Spirit does not want me to spend the rest of my life grieving over what I lost because of the hurts from my relationship with my mother. Instead, He wants to make it up to me for what I missed out on, through no fault of my own. I know this is how the Holy Spirit feels about me, and each of His sons and daughters, because He tells me so in His own words...

> *"I will gasp and pant like a woman giving birth...*
>
> *I will lead you down a new path.*
> *I will guide you along an unfamiliar way.*
> *I will make the darkness bright before you*
> *and I will smooth out the road ahead of you.*
> *I will do these things and I will not forsake you."*
> *(Isaiah 42:14-16 NLT)*
> *Personalized*

> *"I will restore your soul."*
> *(Psalm 23:3 NAS)*
> *Personalized*

"I will make it up to you
for the years the locusts have eaten."
(Joel 2:25 NAS)
Personalized

"I will give you back what you lost."
(Joel 2:25 NLT)
Personalized

"I will make you even more prosperous than you were before."
(Ezekiel 36:11 NLT)
Personalized

"I will renew your lost youth like the eagle."
(Psalm 103:5 NAS)
Personalized

"I will turn into good what the enemy
has meant for evil against you."
(Genesis 50:20 NLT)
Personalized

"Comfort, comfort, My child, I say tenderly to you.
Your sad days are gone."
(Isaiah 40:1-2 NLT)
Personalized

"When you walk through the Valley of Weeping,
it will become a place of refreshing springs where
pools of blessing collect after the rains."
(Psalm 84:6 NLT)

"I will transform your Valley of Trouble into a gateway of hope."
(Hosea 2:15 NLT)
Personalized

"I will open rivers on your bare heights
and springs in the midst of your valleys.
I will make your wilderness a pool of water
and your dry land fountains of water.

I will even make a roadway in your wilderness
and rivers in your desert.
I will comfort you.
I will comfort all your waste places.

Your wilderness I will make like Eden.
Your desert like My garden.
Joy and gladness will be found in you.
Thanksgiving and the sound of a melody."
(Isaiah 41:18, 43:19, 51:3 NAS)
Personalized

I will rebuild you.

You will again be happy!"

(Jeremiah 31:4 NLT)
Personalized

The Holy Spirit kept these promises to me. He restored everything that I lost as a result of Mom's rejection. He gave me back my health. He took my wounded, broken heart and gave me a happy one.

He filled my life with so much nurturing and comfort, when I think about my mother, I am not sad anymore. My need for a mother's love is completely provided for in all the gentle ways the Holy Spirit shows me He loves me. He has restored my life so completely, the years of pain have washed away, as if they never happened. They simply do not matter anymore!

Chapter Seven

I must forgive!

No child wants to hate his parents. When I get so hurt that I end up hating my Mom or Dad, something inside me dies that I need in order to be a whole person. The death of that part of me remains, until I forgive.

If I refuse to forgive, my bitterness is deadly!

As with any sin, bitterness creates a barrier between the Lord and myself. If I persist in my bitterness, I give God no choice. He is not able to be close to me. He can't fellowship with me like He longs to do. He can't send His answers to my prayers. He can't help me and He is the only one who can!

"The prayers of a person,
who ignores the law (God's Word), are despised!"
(Proverbs 28:9 NLT)

"Listen, I'm not too weak to save you, and I'm not becoming deaf.
I can hear you when you call.
But there is a problem-

Your sins have cut you off from Me..
Because of your sin, I have turned away from you and
I will not listen anymore."
(Isaiah 59:1-2 NLT)
Personalized

Bitterness also makes it impossible
for God to forgive me when I need forgiveness.

"You can't get forgiveness from God,
without also forgiving others.
If you refuse to do your part,
you cut yourself off from God's part!"
(Matthew Chapter Six The Message)

Bitterness is so evil,
it sabotages my worship to God.

"If you are standing before the altar in the Temple, offering a
sacrifice to God, and suddenly remember that someone has something
against you, leave your sacrifice there beside the altar. Go and be
reconciled to that person. Then come and offer your sacrifice to God"
(Matthew 5:23-24 NLT).

In fact, the Word calls a person a liar, if he says he loves the
Lord and wants to have fellowship with Him,
yet refuses to forgive.

"We are lying if we say we have fellowship with God
but go on living in spiritual darkness."
(I John 1:6 NLT)

The deadliness of the spiritual darkness caused by bitterness
is graphically captured in the following Scripture:

"Watch out!
See to it that no root of bitterness springs up, causing trouble and
defiling many. For whenever bitterness springs up,
many are corrupted by its poison."
(Hebrews 12:15 NLT/NAS)
Personalized

The word defile has a sobering meaning:

To contaminate, trample, infect by association with, poison, make unfit for use by the introduction of unwholesome or undesirable elements, to make foul what should have been kept clean and pure and held sacred, to make filthy (Webster's New Collegiate Dictionary).

This definition clearly identifies the evil of unforgiveness. It not only causes trouble in the life of the bitter person. It also infects those close to him with its deadly poison.

If I am so hurt that I feel incapable of taking the first step towards forgiving, there is hope! God promises to help me have the strength to make that decision.

"Cry out to Me for help and I will put you back together. I will pull you out of the grave and give you another chance at life."
(Psalm 30 The Message)
Personalized

"Cry out to Me for help and I will heal you."
(Psalm 30:2 NLT/NAS)
Personalized

"I will lift the yoke of slavery from your neck so that you can walk free with your head held high."
(Levitcus 26:13 NLT)
Personalized

Until I let God help me forgive, I will not be free of the past. I cannot get on with the rest of my life. I become mired in perpetually analyzing my "abuse issues". This negative focus can become so addictive, I get stuck in the cesspool of my childhood victimization. Dwelling on past hurts becomes a destructive, self-defeating lifestyle.

I made this mistake.

By the time I was thirty-two years old, I had been a Christian almost two years. I had received excellent teaching on the necessity of forgiveness. Yet, I foolishly hung on to my hatred of Mom. That decision catapulted me to the brink of a serious breakdown.

In a matter of a few weeks, my world came crashing down all around me. I heard voices, but no one was actually speaking to me. Late at night, I was afraid to walk past the livingroom if the lights weren't turned on. I was sure someone was lurking in the shadows, waiting to attack me. Inevitably, I rushed to turn on the lights, but no one was ever there.

I often awoke in a cold sweat from terrifying nightmares. In my dreams, my ex-husband stalked me. He kept coming back to kill me.

During the day, a chilling apprehension obsessed me. I shuddered with fear every time my children walked outside to play. Thoughts of them being killed haunted me.

I was especially troubled whenever someone walked up to the front door.

One morning, I heard a persistent knock. I stood, paralyzed, a few feet from the bolted door. The person knocked again, more insistently. I was too frightened to respond.

"It could be my ex-husband," I told myself. "He's come back to hurt me."

I waited, anxiously, for the person to leave. Eventually, he gave up.

Relieved, I retreated to my bedroom. Moments later, as I lay on my bed, I was convinced that a man was coming stealthily down the hallway towards my room. My heart raced. My body stiffened under the cold sheets. I was too terrified to make a sound.

I strained to listen for footsteps. The room was silent, except for my muffled breathing. I pulled the blanket tight up under my chin and stared, intently, at the partially opened door.

"He's going to kill me," I told myself, frantically clutching the blanket. "I know there's someone out there and he's going to kill me!"

I waited. Finally I realized that no one was there!

"I am going crazy," I thought, hysterically.

The long, sick history of generations in both sides of my family who were mentally ill or who had gone insane raced through my mind. "I'm going to end up just like one of them. I'm losing my mind."

"Oh God," I cried out. "Help me. Please help me."

His response was immediate.

"Ruth," He told me, firmly. "You must forgive your mother. That is the bitter root that is destroying you."

"After all she has done to me," I told the Lord, vehemently, "I have every right to hate her. I'll forgive everyone else, but I will never forgive Mom – never!"

Once again, God spoke clearly to me.

"If you don't forgive her," He warned me. "Your hatred will destroy you and I won't be able to protect you from its destruction."

I jumped up from my bed and stood in the middle of the room, shaking with loud sobs. I could not go on living the way I was feeling. I knew that reality was dangerously close to slipping away from my grasp.

"Oh God," I cried out. "Please help me! I don't feel any forgiveness towards Mom, but I will do what You are telling me to do. Help me, please, to feel that way about her in my heart."

Frightened and desperate, I lifted my arms up to the Lord, just as a young, trusting child would reach out to her father.

"I forgive her, Lord," I said, in a strained voice. "I forgive her....."

At first, I said these words completely by faith. Then, as I spoke them over and over, my feelings towards my mother made a startling change.

Scenes from my childhood flashed through my mind. I recalled Mom bending over the kitchen sink, moaning in pain; Mom lying stiff and white as a corpse on her bed in her darkened room, her countenance clouded with despair; Mom collapsed on the kitchen floor, unable to speak. My heart ached for her as I saw her for the first time through the eyes of Jesus. I felt her sadness, her overwhelming hopelessness.

"She knew I was suffering, but she was drowning in too much pain herself to have anything to give to me," I realized.

"Yes, I forgive Mom," I told the Lord, relieved. "I not only forgive her, I finally can say I love her."

That night, I slept peacefully. The voices in my head were silenced. The shadows in my home were just that, harmless shadows. The infection of my bitterness was gone.

The barrier between God and me came down. Mom never looked the same to me. My hatred of her had been permanently replaced with a tender compassion.

Many years have passed since I took that crucial step of forgiving my mother. Although she never treated me any differently, I moved on, from that point, and changed dramatically.

I have a wonderful "Dad" in "Papa God" and the best "Mom" in the whole world in the Holy Spirit. I have a happy, fulfilling life. I am married to a man who treats me with a gentle, kind love every day of our marriage.

God has done what He said He would do:

"I say to you, a prisoner of darkness,

'Come out!

I am giving you your freedom'."

(Isaiah 49:9 NLT)
Personalized

Yet, none of this amazing restoration would have been possible, if I had continued to pollute my life with hatred.

Part Three

Facing the Present:

The changes I need to make!

Chapter Eight

My Choices vs. Blaming Others

**To break the cycle of abuse in my life,
I had to face this truth:**

*My life is a mess, not because of someone else,
but because of my own wrong choices.*

It is true that *"Children suffer for their parents' sins" (Jeremiah 32:18 NLT)*. Innocent, defenseless children are, in fact, victimized by abusive parents. Their suffering is tragic and heartbreaking. The scars from the abuse can seriously affect them far into adulthood. I definitely was one of those victimized children.

However, a great deal of contemporary psychology tells these hurting adults:

"You are a victim of what someone else has done to you. Let's analyze how you were victimized. In the process, you'll need years of professional therapy. It is also essential that you never miss your psychology-based support group. Your full recovery is very much dependent on you being there. You will learn from the other people how to recover from what was done to you.

If you don't get this professional therapy for your victimization issues and you don't get involved in one of these groups, I doubt, seriously, that you will make it!"

For a Christian, there are several serious errors in this popular approach to overcoming emotional pain.

I am trained to perceive myself as a victim, rather than as an adult who must take full responsibility for his choices.

I blame others, who have abused me, for my problems. In doing so, personal accountability, that is stressed in God's Word, is discarded as irrelevant.

I get my answers about how to deal with the issues in my life from the people in a secular support group. Humanistic solutions to my problems become the basis for my "recovery", rather than the answers in God's Word that have supernatural power to heal me.

Sad to say, this approach to personal counseling has gradually become an entrenched stronghold in many churches today. For these churches, the Bible is no longer the standard used to counsel hurting people and troubled marriages. Instead, human reasoning and secular psychology are on the throne.

This grieves the heart of God.

Yes, professional, psychological help is necessary sometimes, even advisable. However, God's primary provision for the help that I need from other people is in His church.

God never intended that I travel alone on my journey towards the healing that I seek. Such isolation is deadly. It is treacherous. It leaves me dangerously vulnerable to every attack and deception from Satan, the enemy of my soul. Therefore, God has a practical plan to release all this healing power into my life.

He created each of His children with a built-in need for genuine, caring fellowship with one another. His plan is that, as members of His family, we find strength in each other's Jesus-centered support. Through healthy personal relationships with other Christians, we can *speak the truth in love" (Ephesians 4:15 NAS Personalized)* to each other. In doing so, we can challenge each other to explore new places of personal growth.

We can receive invaluable, inspiring insights during times of group ministry that focus on the solutions to my struggles that are found in God's Word.

Through teachings on spiritual warfare, we can learn how to walk in our full spiritual authority over all the forces of evil.

We can be the embrace of Jesus to each other, during times of unbearable pain.

For these reasons, God exhorts us not to neglect coming together, so that we can *"encourage one another" (Hebrews 10:25 NAS)*. In fact, a powerful reason He *"comforts and strengthens us in our hardships and trials is so that when others are troubled and are in need of encouragement, we can pass on to them the same help and comfort He has given to us" (II Corinthians 1:3-5 TLB Personalized)*.

This Word-based, Holy-Spirit-anointed encouragement can ignite the miracle of God's healing in another person's life. It can change a troubled soul, forever!

* * *

I spent years searching for answers to my pain. I longed to live the breakthrough that Paul describes in Philippians 3:13. I yearned to be able to forget what was behind me and effectively press forward to God's destined purpose for my life. Yet, the fulfillment of that destiny was always, seemingly, just out of reach. I ached to be able to make this transition without the emotional baggage that always succeeded in defeating me.

Despite wanting, so earnestly, to be whole I ended up in disheartening dead-ends and frustrating ditches. With the best of intentions, I repeatedly chose detours that devoured precious years of my life.

Then, finally, I understood two simple truths that somehow had escaped me. Grasping them set me free from some of my most crippling shackles:

I can't change what happened to me in the past, but I have the power to choose how I will respond to it in the present! That choice, according to God's Word, is what determines if my present life is a *'blessing or a curse'*.

"Now listen!

*Today I am giving you a choice
between prosperity and disaster.*

I set before you life and death, the blessing and the curse.

*So choose life in order that you may live,
you and your descendants!"*

(Deuteronomy 30:15,19 NLT/NAS)

**I also finally understood:
Other people can only do to me what I allow them to do!**

When I stopped blaming other people for what *"they had done to me"* and I took responsibility for what I allowed, I took a giant step toward becoming a whole person! I stopped looking at myself as an adult victim! I saw my present condition as the sum total of my own destructive choices. Then, with God's help, I began to take control of my life and my choices.

In other words...

I can choose to forgive.

I can choose to *"fix my thoughts on what is pure, lovely and admirable...I can decide to think about what is excellent and worthy of praise"* (Philippians 4:8 NLT Personalized).

I can decide to learn all that I can learn about my authority as a believer and stop letting Satan beat me up with his attacks and oppression.

I can choose to make it a high priority to get to know God as my real "Dad" and the Holy Spirit as my Comforter.

I can diligently study God's Word and learn what He says about who I am. Then I can consciously decide to put behind me the cruel words that were spoken into my life. From that point, I can decide that my new identity is based completely on who my "Abba Father" tells me I am and no longer on the voices of the past.

I can make these positive, healing choices and be blessed or I can make choices that will continue to imprison me in my pain.

I can neglect times of intimacy with God.

I can make it a low priority to study His Word.

I can choose to be isolated from fellowship with His people.

I can decide to hang on to my bitterness that *"I have every right to feel"*.

I can continue to define who I am through the words of those who abused me.

I can choose to think about every rotten thing that has ever been done or said to me, in all their agonizing details.

I can do, as I have always done, and allow others to be abusive, cruel and controlling towards me. Having made that destructive choice, I can then keep on blaming those people for the misery in my life.

If these are my choices, I prolong my suffering. I totally frustrate God's power to heal me! I choose a curse and not a blessing for my life and I have done it to myself.

When my first abusive marriage ended, I did not have these insights. I mistakenly told myself:

> *"I just got rid of my problem!*
> *My abusive husband is out of my life,*
> *so now everything is going to be all right."*

Within a year, I remarried.

This marriage proved to be far more damaging than the first one! Even though I convinced myself that I had learned enough from my first marriage to make the right decision about a second one, I ended up in another abusive relationship.

The only difference was, my first husband beat me with his fists. This man's "blows" were his cruel words towards me and my children.

When this marriage ended, fourteen years later, my attitude was totally different. This time I asked myself,

> *"Why am I attracted to abusive men*
> *and why are they attracted to me?*
>
> *What do I need to do to break this cycle of*
> *being drawn, over and over, into*
> *destructive relationships?"*

My thoughts were no longer focused on blaming someone else for *"what he did to me"*. Instead, I was determined to understand how I needed to change so that my pattern of choosing abusive relationships would not be repeated.

If I had not made this transition in my thinking, from blaming others to personal responsibility for my choices and for what I allow, I would have inevitably made the same disastrous mistake again. I would have eventually ended up in a third abusive marriage!

Chapter Nine

Love is not taking on someone else's pain as my own!

A healthy person is not comfortable letting me take responsibility for what he knows he should be doing for himself! He does not want me to "feel sorry for him". He does not want me to "take care of him", because he knows full well, as an adult, that he should be taking care of himself.

We all have days when we need the emotional support of the other person in a close relationship and that person has days when he needs my emotional support. That's a healthy exchange of mutual love and caring! However, a healthy person does not want to become dependent on me for his emotional needs.

Before I learned the importance of not taking on someone else's pain as my own, I allowed dependent people to lean on me with their problems. In doing so, I encouraged them to manipulate me and use me as their emotional garbage dump. They felt better, momentarily, and I became weighted down and worn out with their "stuff". I became a magnet for people who were unwilling to accept personal responsibility for looking to the Lord and His Word to resolve their overloads. This need for sympathy, without personal accountability, is a common characteristic of the abusive personality.

I established this pattern of letting people lean on me, emotionally, at a young age. I was praised when I mothered other people in the family. I was noticed whenever I helped one of them with their problems. The only time I felt valued was when I was needed. Consequently, I learned to define love as someone needing me.

When I became a Christian, I continued this learned behavior. I mistakenly thought I was following God's instruction to love people. Only after suffering twenty-one years in two devastating marriages did I finally realize the error of my thinking. The following insights from God's Word illuminated my understanding.

The Bible instructs me, *"If one member suffers, all the members suffer with it...care for one another"* (I Corinthians 12:26 NAS). This *"caring for one another"* is a healthy Biblical empathy for what someone else is experiencing. It is not referring to internalizing that person's pain and making it my own.

The Bible also tells me to *"Bear one another's burdens"* (*Galatians 6:2 NAS*). At first glance, this verse appears to be reinforcing my conditioning to become emotionally involved, to an unhealthy degree, in another person's pain and struggles. However, Galatians 6:2 is actually saying: *"Help another person with their overload by letting them know I care."*

Galatians 6:2 is not saying: *"Carry someone's overload and get emotionally burdened down with it myself."* This approach has no power to effectively help the other person. It only ends up transferring their burden to me.

God's Word makes it clear exactly *where* the person who is burdened is supposed to cast his overload and it's not on me.

"Humble yourselves...casting all your anxiety upon Him
(and not on another person)
because He cares for you."
(I Peter 5:7 NAS)

"Cast your burden upon the Lord,
(and not on another person)
and He will sustain you."
(Psalm 55:22 NAS)

The Word gives me these directives because it is *"the Lord who lifts the burden of those bent beneath their loads"* *(Psalm 146:8 NLT)*.

Therefore, when someone else is hurting my message to them needs to be: *"I can't fix your problem. The only thing I can do is direct you to the Person who can. If you don't want to go there, there is nothing else I can do for you."*

I found it extremely eye-opening when I first noticed that three verses after Galatians 6:2 instructs me to *"bear one another's burdens"* I am told in Galatians 6:5 that *"each one shall bear his own load"*.

In other words, I am to be moved with compassion by the suffering of others. I am to be practical in my expression of love towards them. I am to be that embrace of Jesus to my brothers and sisters in the Lord during their times of unbearable pain. I am to celebrate their joys and *"weep with those who weep"*. Yet, the built-in, Biblical balance for this compassionate love is the directive in Galatians 6:5 to *"each bear his own load"*. In other words, each of us is accountable for our own well being, choices and struggles. Ultimately, each of us is responsible for our own *"load"*. The different versions of Galatians 6:5 make this point even more clear:

" We are each responsible for our own conduct."
(Galatians 6:5 NLT)

"Each of us must take responsibility for doing the creative best we can with our own life."
(Galatians 6:5 The Message)

I now adhere to this Biblical perspective in my interactions with people. As a result, I can detect when a person wants to lean on me to an unhealthy degree and I do not allow it.

I also can watch an adult struggle, with whom I have a close relationship. Yet, I do not feel it is my responsibility to relieve the pressure he is under. I do not try to resolve his struggle for him.

I know he is suffering, but I don't try to figure out how I can take away his pain.

I tell myself, and honestly mean it:

"I care about this person. I care that he is hurting. I support him. I will exercise the full authority Jesus gives me as His child and pray for this person.

But this pain is his pain. It does not belong to me. I will not feel responsible to take ownership of it, as if it were my own. I respect that he is a separate person from me. He is an adult who is having a hard time. He is not a hurting, helpless child.

I can't resolve his pain for him. I fully realize that I will not be responding in a healthy way if I try to do so.

Therefore, I step back, in my emotional involvement, and let him work it through himself, while I continue praying, loving and being genuinely supportive and caring towards him in a Biblically sound way."

I have found that healthy people want to be treated in this way. They have a teachable heart before the Lord. They are willing to do whatever it takes to grow, no matter what they are facing. They are responsive to the Lord telling them what to do through His Word and through sound, Bible-based teaching and counseling.

I have also learned that people who have no intentions of taking responsibility for their own life and issues are offended, even repelled, by my setting healthy boundaries in my interactions with them. For example, when I am unwilling to be available to them as their emotional "garbage dump", their perception is often that I am unwilling to do enough to "help" them. The truth is when I set boundaries in my involvement with people I am operating in God's wisdom.

Chapter Ten

Be aware!
Control leads to abuse!

**To avoid abusive relationships,
or to end abuse in a present relationship,
it is essential to understand:**

*A controlling person is always
one step away from being abusive.*

*As soon as a controlling person can no longer control
me, that is when the abuse can begin!*

God's Word gives this sobering warning:
"You are a slave to whatever controls you."
(II Peter 2:19 NLT)

That slavery includes me allowing any person to become my "master", because I relinquish to him the power to be controlling over me. God is the only Person to whom I am to surrender control over my life! When I give it to anyone else, I throw away the freedom Jesus died to give me:

"I have paid the price to set you free!"
(Isaiah 44:22 NLT)

Therefore, I must evaluate, honestly, all the relationships in my life. I must identify any that are controlling. I then must be determined to do whatever it takes to not allow anyone to be controlling over me again. To be controlled is unhealthy. Therefore, I have to decide that to be controlled is unacceptable!

"Because of the cross of Jesus,
I have been set free from the stifling atmosphere
of pleasing others and fitting into the little patterns that they dictate.
Can't you see the central issue in all this?
It is not what you and I do. It is what God is doing,
and He is creating something totally new, a free life!"
(Galatians Chapter Six The Message)
Personalized

"Don't tolerate people who try to run your life!"
(Colossians Chapter Two The Message)

Some examples of behaviors
that are clear indications a person is controlling:

I have to like what he thinks I should like. I have to do what he thinks I should do. I have to be who he thinks I should be. If I differ with him in any of these areas, as far as he is concerned, there is something wrong with me. He cannot be the one who is wrong.

I have to live up to his expectations or he can't handle it. If I am anything less than what he expects, he is critical and disapproving. I am a disappointment to him.

If I make a decision that he does not agree with, he will withdraw his support from me.

He displays anger, even rage, when I express an insight or point of view that is different from his.

He has to be right in any disagreement, even if it is blatantly obvious that he is wrong. To be wrong is to lose some of his control. Therefore, being right is the most important thing to him. This overriding need to always be right causes him to be rigid, stubborn, set in his ways, all of which makes healthy communication and conflict resolution impossible.

He is verbally abusive. Words have power! When his words are cruel, he is able to provoke a response out of me that puts him in control of my emotions.

He demands that I treat him with respect, but he does not give that same respect to me. The reason is quite simple! The only opinion he values is his own. The only way of doing things that he genuinely respects is his way! Therefore, he has no basic respect for what I think or how I feel, unless, of course, I am in full agreement with him.

He degrades me in front of our children or other people and feels fully justified in doing so.

He uses the Bible to validate his demanding, selfish, rude, unkind or dominating behaviors.

He is self-righteous about his Christianity and critical of mine. His interpretation of the Bible is "right" and he dismisses my interpretation as not worthy of consideration.

His puts a heavy emphasis on the Scriptures that supposedly support his position of power and control over me, including in the sexual area.

Money is power. Absolute control of the money gives him tremendous power over me. Therefore, he uses money to try to control me. He withholds money from me to retaliate against me for not doing what he wants. He uses giving me money as a leverage to get what he wants out of me.

He insists that it is "none of my business" how money is being spent. He holds a tight rein on all spending. He does not include me in the decisions about how money is spent.

He tries to control what I do with my time.

He can't be happy for me if I am enjoying a hobby or experiencing a success that does not involve him. He feels he is losing part of his control over me. He tries to ' sabotage my hobbies and areas of enjoyment and success that don't involve him.

He tries to control who my friends are and attempts to alienate me from the people he does not want me to be friends with.

When I ask him for input or suggestions, he is upset if I don't abide by what he tells me. His suggestions carry the weight of commands.

His world evolves around his needs and his feelings. If something affects his needs or his feelings, he is sensitive to it. It becomes a high priority. If it just affects me, it is not a priority. A controlling person, therefore, is intrinsically selfish. He is centered in, almost exclusively, on himself.

Chapter Eleven

I can't make another person happy!

**To function in a healthy way in any relationship,
I must remind myself often:**

*It is not my responsibility
to make another person happy.*

An unhealthy person, who is depressed, miserable and views life from a chronically negative perspective, often has the expectation that somehow it is my responsibility to do something to make him happy. However, any efforts I invest to improve his "happiness level" can be compared to me pouring water into a bucket with holes in it. As fast as I pour into that person, whatever good he experiences drains right back out of him. Even if my efforts help temporarily, that benefit inevitably fades. Then he is right back where he started — negative, miserable and expecting me to feel pressured to do something about it.

Likewise, it is not the responsibility of anyone else to make me happy. Happiness is something I need to trust God to help me find within my own heart and spirit towards myself. That happiness comes from a healthy self-love. It comes from letting God get through to me, on a daily basis, how tenderly and deeply He loves me. It comes from reminding myself, often, no matter what the circumstances are that surround me:

"To God, I am precious. I am special. I am worth so much to Him that He came and died for me so that I could be whole and at peace!"

*God's Word makes it clear
that is exactly how He feels about me....*

"*You are precious to Me. You are honored and I love you.*"
(Isaiah 43:4 NLT)

"*I have chosen you for Myself, for My own special treasure.*"
(Psalm 135:4 NLT)
Personalized

"*You are close to My heart.*"
(Psalm 148:14 NIV)
Personalized

"*I declare today that you are My own special treasure.*"
(Deuteronomy 26:18 NLT)
Personalized

If my happiness is based on how other people feel about me, my emotions will rise and fall with all the variations in my relationships.

In sharp contrast, if my happiness is rooted in God's unchanging love for me, it weathers the storms of life with amazing peace. No matter what happens in any of my relationships, I can always come back to this thought, with absolute certainty:

Lord, I am special to You. I am loved by You.

I am close to Your heart.

No matter what, I am Your treasure!

I learned this lesson the hard way.

When I met my second husband, I was a single mom with the full responsibility of providing for two young children. I had no financial support. My previous husband disappeared shortly after the marriage ended. I had no skills to get a job that would provide me with an adequate income. I was scared. I wanted my "prince charming" to come along and rescue me from all these overwhelming pressures.

I did not slow down and let God teach me how to be happy within myself. I did not choose to trust Him to help me pull my life together. Instead, I foolishly thought a relationship was the solution to my problems. I wanted a man to come into my life who could make me happy. Consequently, I rushed into a second marriage.

By the time that second marriage ended, fourteen years later, I had "grown up" emotionally. I no longer accepted the responsibility to try to make someone else happy. I also no longer expected someone else to make me happy. I understood that other people can only enhance the happiness I have found within myself.

As a result of the years of struggling and growing, I now felt so loved, so special, so treasured by the Lord, I was no longer dependent on someone else to give me those feelings. Instead, I had learned to live in the steady reality of how God feels about me. When the storms of life hit, I now reminded myself of His unchanging love for me. Contrary to all the years I lived on an emotional roller coaster, whenever I felt the slightest rejection, His constant love became the basis for my emotional stability and my resounding inner peace.

Chapter Twelve

I need to listen to the "red flags"!

**To protect myself from getting involved
in another abusive relationship,
I must decide:**

*I will never again ignore the Holy Spirit
trying to warn me that a relationship is unhealthy,
destructive, abusive or controlling.*

*I will no longer want a relationship so desperately,
that I ignore the "red flags".*

When my first marriage ended, I cried out to God to help me make the right decisions about any future relationships. I had already suffered enough from my bad choices. Yet, I still ended up in another sick marriage.

I suffered for fourteen years in a second marriage that God never intended for me. I did so because I did not understand the absolute necessity of taking seriously the blatant indications that this relationship was a mistake!

For a long time, I felt betrayed by God.

"Why didn't you warn me, Lord?" I cried out. *"I don't understand! I trusted You. I prayed. And here I am in another mess!"*

God did warn me I was marching into another disastrous mistake, but I was in such denial, I did not want to see His "red flags". The cycle of abusive relationships was too deeply embedded in the fabric of how I perceived life and people.

During the months prior to the wedding, I dismissed every blaring signal that this man was controlling, stubborn, selfish, stingy and insensitive to my needs. I had no understanding, whatsoever, that he was the classic "needy" person.

His whole personality and all of his behaviors cried out, whenever I was with him:

"Take care of me. Feel sorry for me. I am down (a lot!) so I need you to make me happy."

From the very beginning, this man acted secretive about money. Once we were married, money became the sickest way I allowed him to control me. He hated women. He especially harbored a deep resentment towards his controlling, dominating mother, who had never treated his manhood with any respect. It was also obvious that his family did not approve of me as his choice for a wife. Their response to me was immediately cold and rejecting.

You may be saying, and understandably so,

"How can anyone who knows the Lord be that stupid? How can anyone be that blind?

How could anyone, who is praying about a relationship, marry someone who exhibited all of these negative traits before she married him?"

The answer is simple. I wanted a relationship so desperately, I blocked out all of the Holy Spirit's efforts to get my attention about the problems. Consequently, no matter how much I prayed and asked God to help me, I was blinded by my own impenetrable denial!

Some of the behaviors that are automatic "red flags" in any relationship:

On my part...

The relationship is affecting my health.

I feel controlled.

I feel stifled, smothered.

I am not comfortable introducing him to my friends.

I feel used, or worse yet, degraded, when I am around him.

I don't feel free to be completely myself when I am around him. I don't feel like I can totally relax and "let my hair down" with him.

I find myself frequently walking on "egg shells", when I am around him. I am concerned about how he will react to me.

I protect him from my true feelings. In doing so, I act like he is a child, who cannot handle my honest feelings.

I allow him to be dominating over me, to tell me what to do. In doing so, I am acting as a "child". I am allowing this person to relate to me as my "parent".

I am becoming so emotionally involved with his problems that I am feeling burdened by them. I feel a responsibility to help him "fix" his problems.

I make excuses for his behaviors to other people and to myself.

I find myself becoming more and more isolated from other people I am close to.

On his part...

He does not "take it to heart" when I tell him that his behaviors towards me are hurtful, troubling, unkind, etc.

He is demanding.

He expects me to "wait on him".

He bristles, if I ask him to help me.

He is stingy. He is extremely private about his money.

He is selfish and self-centered.

He is oblivious to my feelings or needs.

He is dominating.

He is moody.

He exhibits anti-social behavior around other people.

He has sudden mood swings and unpredictable behaviors.

He is easily upset by annoyances that are a part of daily life.

He is emotionally dependent on me. He leans on me for his emotional needs instead of taking responsibility for them himself.

He is often depressed. He frequently expresses a gloomy, negative perspective about life.

He does not like himself. He is insecure in who he is. His self-confidence is so shaky, my strengths and my successes easily threaten him.

He does most of the talking in our conversations. He does not reciprocate by making it a priority to listen to me.

He is sullen and quiet. He is non-communicative because he buries his true feelings deep inside of him.

He has a quick excuse for being rude, unkind, selfish, etc. He explains away negative behaviors and expects me to accept his rationalizations and excuses.

He dwells on past relationships and past hurts. He has not let go of the hurts of the past. He is bitter. He is a grudge holder!

He is quick to blame others for his past problems rather than taking personal responsibility for them himself.

He is quick to blame me, if we have problems. Everything is "my fault".

His response to conflict between us is to be defensive, to verbally attack me, refuse to listen to me, shut down on me emotionally or shut me out.

He makes promises, but he doesn't keep his word to me.

He says he is a Christian. He talks about Jesus. But there is no fruit in his life. He isn't "walking his talk"!

He feels inadequate a lot of the time. I find myself constantly in the role of reassuring him, encouraging him, "pumping up" his low self-esteem.

He is looking for someone to rescue him from his situation or personal problems.

He is looking for someone to take care of him.

He is critical of me.

He wants to change me.

He puts me down, privately or in front of other people.

He is jealous of my time with other people. He pressures me to distance myself from my support system, such as friends, co-workers, close family members.

He has to be in control.

He insists on helping me make personal decisions.

He tries to control what I do with my money.

He tries to control whom I spend my time with.

He loses his temper easily. When he does, I feel uneasy.

It has crossed my mind that, due to the intensity of his anger, he could be someone whose anger could get out of control. That thought is scary to me.

He breaks or strikes objects, when he gets angry.

He has hit other people in the past and has excuses why "they pushed him over the edge".

Although he hasn't physically hit me, he makes verbal threats of violence, such as, "I'll slap you".

He has hit me and is profusely sorry. He promises it will never happen again.

As a couple...

Physical pleasure in the relationship is the number one focus. No real friendship is developing.

We have very little in common in our goals or interests. We are mainly opposites in the way we think, which gives us a lot to argue about.

Once I decide to listen to the Holy Spirit giving me warning signals in any relationship, I need to remember that God cautions me:

"Be shrewd as serpents and innocent as doves."
(Matthew 10:16 NAS)

This godly shrewdness is the diametric opposite of denial, which is *"a refusal to admit the truth" (Webster's New Collegiate Dictionary)*. Denial blinds me to reality. It causes me to create my own reality, that is far removed from the truth about another person. Therefore, to *"be shrewd as a serpent"* in relationships, I need to face, head on, any shred of denial that still is operating in my thinking.

God wants to help me make this transition out of denial into sound judgment. The good news is that He wants this for me, even more than I do! As long as I am willing to listen to Him, He is more than able to keep me going in a healthy direction and give me a clear understanding of the truth. He is fully able to reveal to me insights about life and people that, apart from His help, I would not be able to see.

If I ever revert back to my old habit of blocking out objective reality, God is always available to help me get back on the right track. He will give me every bit of discernment I need to see another person for who he really is. He will gladly help me succeed in the changes I am trying to make. I simply must be willing to listen to Him and then act on the wisdom He gives me.

"Call out to Me and I will answer you.
I will answer you by revealing to you what is hard and hidden,
those things that you do not know."
(Jeremiah 33:3 Moffatt)
Personalized

"The revelation of God is whole and pulls our lives together.
The signposts of God are clear and point out the right road.
The life-maps of God are right, showing the way to joy.
The directions from God are plain!"
(Psalm 19 The Message)

"He corrects the misdirected and sends them in the right direction."
(Psalm 25 The Message)

"Listen for God's Voice in everything you do, everywhere you go.
He's the one who will keep you on track!"
(Proverbs Chapter Three The Message)

"The Lord says,
' I will guide you along the best pathway for your life.
I will advise you and watch over you.'"
(Psalm 32:8 NLT)

Lord, "I still belong to You.
You are holding my right hand.
You will keep on guiding me with Your counsel,
leading me to a glorious destiny!"
(Psalm 73:23-24 NLT)

Chapter Thirteen

I can't change another person!

To stop any pattern of choosing disastrous relationships, I must decide I will not look at someone I am considering dating or marrying and tell myself:

I see his potential as a person.
If I just love him enough or if I do this or that for him, he will change.

The way a person treats me does not improve after I marry him, no matter how much I pour my love into him. As a spouse, he will only be the way he was when I met him, only more so.

When I first met my second husband, I was energized by the potential for growth that I saw in him. Consequently, his weaknesses and personality flaws only made him that much more attractive to me.

He was stingy with his money, but I was convinced that I would try so hard to be good to him, he would learn to be generous. He was excessively nervous. I decided I would be so understanding and kind to him, his nervousness would heal. His home was filthy and chaotic. I convinced myself that he just needed a wife to keep a pretty house for him. He would be so grateful that I made our home lovely, he would treat it totally different from the glaringly neglected home he lived in as a bachelor. I noticed he was bitter towards women, but I was certain he would never feel that way about me!

"He's got a lot of rough edges," I told myself. "But if I just love him and encourage him enough, if I do whatever I can do to 'help' him grow, he will be able to make the necessary changes that he needs to make for us to be happy. He has so much untapped potential as a person. His problem is that no one, up to this point in his life, has encouraged him enough to help him develop to that full potential."

Consequently, this man became my "project" to love into changing! I was going to be the one who succeeded, where all others had failed. As a result of this twisted line of reasoning, this "project" had long-term consequences.

The "changes" he made all faded as soon we were married. His stinginess about money turned into a major way he tried to be controlling as early in the marriage as the second day of our honeymoon. His nervousness never improved. Instead, it became even more pronounced. It manifested in his chronic inability to relax and enjoy life. He turned areas in our home into the same dirty chaos that he lived in when I first met him.

His disdain towards women, I soon realized, included me also.

From this disillusioning experience, I learned that any changes a person makes to please a future spouse are meaningless. The way a person actually is on the day that I meet him is who he really is. It is unhealthy, to the "max", to fool myself into thinking any changes will last after I marry him.

To avoid making this mistake in any relationship, I must be determined to see any person, whom I am considering dating or marrying, as he really is and not what he could be. I must never allow myself to think:

"Being married to me will change him!"

I also must be *"shrewd as a serpent"*, and not consider entering into a marriage with someone who promises me, *"I will change."*

Chapter Fourteen

I am worthy of being loved!

**To become a whole person,
who can establish healthy relationships,
I must decide:**

I am worthy of being loved.
I am lovable because God tells me I am...

*"You are precious in My sight...
you are honored and I love you"
(Isaiah 43:4 NAS)*

Because I am so precious to the Lord, I deserve to be treated with kindness, respect, tenderness and love. Never again can it be acceptable to allow anyone to be cruel to me.

Instead, I will do exactly what God's Word says:

*"You are not to associate with anyone
who claims to be a Christian, yet ... is abusive.
Don't even eat with such people!"
(I Corinthians 5:11 NLT)*

The revelation that *"I am worthy to be loved!"* is basic. Yet, if I end up in one abusive relationship after another, I am not convinced of this simple truth. If I really believed I was worthy of being loved, I would never again allow anyone to abuse me!

I recall, vividly, the exact moment I made that decision.

It was during the last year of my second marriage. I sat in a chair across from my husband in our bedroom. He sat on the bed and leaned, stiffly, against the wall behind him. In icy silence, he waited for me to speak.

"I am so unhappy in this marriage," I began, my voice quaking with emotion. "I am struggling with thoughts about wanting to die."

I paused, hoping to see some indication that he cared how intensely I was suffering. He simply nodded his head to indicate he heard me.

"If I don't die," I continued, my body trembling with nervousness, "then I find myself wishing you would die so that I could be free. I don't know how much longer I can hurt in this marriage."

He stared at me, coldly. I had invested almost fourteen years of my life trying to love this man. His coldness stung. He made no movement towards me to comfort me. He offered no response to my anguish.

"After all these years, I am convinced you have never loved me," I continued, in a strained, hurt voice.

"You are probably right. I probably never have," he replied, with no emotion.

At that moment, I made a proclamation that I knew, as I spoke it, would have a profound impact on the rest of my life...

"I will no longer be willing to do all the loving and giving in any relationship," I began, emphatically, as I stood up.

"For the first time, I really do believe I am a loveable person. I deserve to be treated with love and kindness. I am worthy to be loved! I will never again accept being treated cruelly by you or anyone.

I walked quietly, confidently, out of the room. I knew that, no matter what price I had to pay, I would never allow anyone to abuse me again.

In the months following that decision, I struggled to understand what God expected of me. My husband and I had spent most of our fourteen years in professional and pastoral counseling, but the problems continued, unchanged. I had tried separation, but any improvement in our relationship rapidly disappeared once we came back together. I had prayed for years for the marriage to be healed, yet it steadily deteriorated. Most troubling of all, my heart ached over the damage my children had suffered from the abuse in our home.

The constant stress in the marriage took its toll on my physical health.

Six months went by. Then, a final incident erupted. I stood in the center of our livingroom and faced my husband.

"That is the last time," I declared to him, just before I walked out the door, "that I will ever allow you to abuse me again!"

I left my husband, that day, and did not return. Yet, I was troubled. I cried out to the Lord to give me peace about ending the marriage. His response to that cry of my heart was both kind and compassionate...

"Picture how a loving father would feel towards his daughter," the Lord ministered to me late one evening.

"This is a father who cherishes his daughter. He loves her dearly. To him, that daughter is his princess. She is exceedingly precious to him. Then one day this daughter calls him on the phone, sobbing hysterically, and reveals to him,

'Dad, my husband is abusing me. He has been doing it for many years. What do I do? I've tried so hard to make this work...I've believed for so long that God could heal this relationship, but now I feel so troubled, I want to die.

And the children, Dad, they've been so hurt. They've suffered so much because of this marriage. Please, Dad, what do I do?' she asked, through her tears.

'I don't want you to stay in this relationship and be destroyed,' the father quickly responded. 'You are too precious to me. Yes, you've tried your best. Yes, you've trusted God and He surely wants to heal this marriage, but neither you nor God have any control over the free will of another person who refuses to change. Now come home. You have a safe place here to heal. I love you so. Come, and let your Mom and me help you. You have suffered long enough.'

"Ruth," the Lord continued, "precious daughter of mine. Remember the scripture...'If a child asks her father for bread, he doesn't trick her with sawdust, does he? If she asks him for fish, he doesn't scare her with a live snake, does he? As bad as you are, you wouldn't do that to your child. So do you think that I, Your Father who conceived you in love, will do that to you' (Matthew Chapter Seven The Message Personalized)?

If an earthly father would not want his daughter to stay in a marriage in which abuse is destroying her and her children, why would you think I would love you any less? If I required of you that you stay, knowing all that I know, I would be a 'monster God' and not your 'Abba Father', who loves you so very much."

I rested my head back against the chair, where I was sitting and closed my eyes. Tension drained out of me. My body relaxed. The turmoil in my spirit left. Finally, I was at peace.

That was the moment when I began a new life on the inside of me. I had spent all of my life *"in a land where death cast its shadow but now I felt like Jesus had just made the sun come up."*

(Matthew Chapter Four The Message/NLT)
Personalized

Chapter Fifteen

I must overcome being "needy"!

**To become a whole, healthy person
who is attracted to whole, healthy people,
I must remind myself, often:**

The less needy I am, the more ready I am to establish a healthy relationship.

How I define *"needy":*

I am unable to feel secure, happy or fulfilled independent of my relationships with other people. If I am not in a relationship, I am miserable.

If I am alone, I am automatically lonely. I feel empty. I feel something essential is missing.

I am so insecure within myself, I am in need of constant affirmation. I am constantly dependent on other people to validate my worth as a person.

There were moments when this decision was difficult. I recall, vividly, one of those times.

I stood, alone, in the middle of my warmly decorated living room. It was hushed, except for the steady ticking of the clock on the wall nearby. God's reassuring Presence was with me in the silence.

I knelt in front of the couch and buried my face in my folded arms. I ached to have someone love me. I longed to have the arms of a man around me, who would be kind towards me. I wanted to be held in the embrace of someone who would love me with the tenderness I had never experienced.

"Please help me, Lord," I cried out. "Please help me!"

I calmed down, as soon as the Lord reminded me of the Scripture He always spoke to me during my most difficult hours as a single woman. I had written the verse and put it in an exquisite, heart shaped frame on a prominent table in the livingroom. I looked up and glanced over at it, as I wiped the tears from my eyes.

> *"Delight yourself in Me and*
> *I will give you the desires of your heart.*
> *Commit your way to Me and trust Me and I will do it!"*
> *(Psalm 37:4-5 NAS)*
> *Personalized*

That was many years ago, now. God kept His Word to me. He gave me all the desires of my heart. He fulfilled every longing. He answered every prayer! All the trust I put in Him and His Word bore lasting fruit.

Today, I am experiencing the joy of a marriage between two healthy partners. There are no control issues in this relationship. There is no abuse. My husband, Barry, is kind to me, always! I am not his mother. He is not my "prince charming" who rescued me from my troubles! He is a man who feels good about himself. Therefore, he doesn't need me to "pump up" his sagging self-esteem!

When we met, neither one of us was *"needy"*. We immediately had fun with each other and that has never changed. Neither one of us can recall a day when we haven't laughed together about something! The day we met, we both liked each other just the way we were. Furthermore, neither one of us would have pursued the relationship, if we felt the other person wanted us to change.

I still chuckle whenever I recall the night we sat in his car and talked, not too long after we began spending time together. We were developing an enjoyable friendship. Yet, there were certain thoughts I promised myself I would express to any man I began to get close to.

"I need to tell you some things about me, Barry!" I began, bluntly, as I turned to face him.

"I will never change for any man again. I will not sacrifice my identity to please another person! I would rather be single the rest of my life than get involved with someone who would expect me to change for him.

God has given me a new life. I am deeply thankful for it. I can walk into my home, now, and be at peace. I can be with Him and not with anyone who is hurting me."

Without pausing or even really considering how my honesty was affecting Barry, I poured out my feelings about men and relationships. Many of the thoughts that I share in this book are what I shared with Barry that evening.

My torrent of words finally ended with this thought:

"I am determined to serve the Lord the rest of my life. No relationship will ever be worth it to me, if I feel I have to sacrifice, in any way, what God wants me to do for Him!

He has called me to serve Him in full-time ministry and that is the most important thing in the world to me! I refuse to lose any more years frustrating that calling. I refuse to take another detour into a relationship with a man who doesn't accept me just the way I am and who can't support me, completely, in how God wants me to serve Him!"

When I finished speaking, I was fully prepared for Barry to tell me, "Ah, nice knowing you. But this probably isn't what I am looking for!"

I was stunned when he turned towards me, with a delightful twinkle in his blue eyes and a pleased grin spread warmly across his face.

"That's just the kind of person I am looking for!" he said without hesitation. "Everything you have said is exactly how I feel too!"

Needless to say, from that point, a deep love rapidly grew between us. The years we have been married have been the happiest years of each of our lives. We treasure each day God gives us to share with each other.

Now that I am experiencing wholeness and peace on a daily basis, I can honestly say that breaking the cycle of abuse was the hardest thing I have had to overcome in my life. The good news is that, by the grace of God and through what I learned from His Word, I have succeeded in doing so.

All the heartache of the past is behind me.   I am a new person! God has given me a completely new life! The way I relate to people is radically different from the years when I surrounded myself with sick, "needy" relationships. God is *"no respecter of persons"* What He has done for me, He makes available to every person who cries out to Him for help!

"Cry to Me for help and I will restore your health.
I do not ignore your suffering. I do not turn and walk away.
I listen to your cries for help. I enjoy helping you."
(Psalm 30:2, 22:24, 35:27 NLT)
Personalized

"I will give you back your health and heal your wounds."
(Jeremiah 30:17 NLT)

"I will be gracious to you, if you ask for My help.
I will respond instantly to the sound of your cries."
(Isaiah 30:19 NLT)
Personalized

Chapter Sixteen

How I know I have changed!

Some of the ways I can tell that I have changed enough to be attracted to a healthy person:

I like who I am.

I have developed a healthy level of independence.

I have a strong confidence that I can take care of my own needs. I am not looking for someone to "take care of me".

I don't have to be in a relationship to be happy and to feel like a whole, complete person.

I can thoroughly enjoy the time I spend alone, with myself.

I have developed my own interests and hobbies.

I have non-romantic friends I can have fun with.

I have my own dreams and goals. I am taking practical steps towards accomplishing them.

The kind of "needy", controlling people who use to be drawn to me are not attracted to me anymore.

I don't feel it's selfish for the loving, giving and supporting to go both ways in a relationship.

I am so convinced that a reciprocal relationship is healthy, anything less than that warns me, loud and clear, that something is seriously wrong.

I don't feel a responsibility to make someone else happy.

I can watch a person, whom I care about, struggle with pain and feel no pressure to take his pain on as if it were my own.

I don't make excuses for unacceptable behaviors, such as someone being selfish, rude, unkind, inconsiderate, controlling.

I have worked through any bitterness or unforgiveness towards anyone who has ever been hurtful or abusive towards me.

I like the person, whom I am getting close to, the way he was the day I met him.   I don't have anything about him that I want to work on helping him to change.

Chapter Seventeen

How I know
I haven't changed enough!

Some of the ways I can tell that
I still will be attracted to an unhealthy person!

I am still energized and motivated by feeling needed by another person. Therefore, I will attract "needy" people who will lean on me for their needs to be met.

I still like to "take care of people" to an extreme. I like to "help" people to an extreme. I tend to "mother" adults. Therefore, I will easily become another person's parent, caretaker, nurturer, therapist and counselor. I will attract a person who is looking for someone to take care of him.

I feel overwhelmed by the pressure of assuming responsibility for my own financial or emotional needs. Therefore, I am vulnerable to wanting someone to come along and rescue me from these pressures and take care of me. I will be drawn to a relationship that is my escape. Consequently, I am not ready for a healthy relationship because a healthy one is always between two people who take responsibility for their own needs and issues.

I feel sorry for people. I see adults, who have been hurt, as victims rather than as people who have choices about how they can respond to what has happened to them. As a result, I am extremely vulnerable to being manipulated into feeling sorry for a person I care about. I will be easily deceived into thinking the pity I feel is love, when it is merely a sick counterfeit.

I want someone to feel sorry for me. Consequently, I will repel a healthy person. Healthy people know better than to get "sucked into" feeling sorry for me!

I just ended an unhealthy relationship and I foolishly think that I am ready to launch right into another close relationship. As a result, I am setting myself up for another disaster! Until I slow down and do some serious "homework" on why I am stuck in a repeated cycle of unhealthy relationships, I will continue to repeat that same pattern! I will continue gravitating to one person after another, who are a serious mistake for my life.

I still dwell on hurts, betrayals and abuse from past relationships. No healthy person is going to be attracted to someone who wants to constantly think and talk about past relationships. Therefore, until I work through my issues from previous relationships, I am not ready to attract a truly healthy person. There is also an alarming probability that, until I change in this area, I will attract other miserable people, who will also dwell on their past hurts.

I still gravitate towards controlling people who want to run my life, instead of people who respect who I am and the decisions I make.

I still have to be in a relationship to feel complete. I can't stand being alone. To be alone is to be lonely.

I still make excuses for behaviors in other people that are unacceptable, such as being unkind, inconsiderate, rude, selfish, stingy, oblivious to my feelings and needs.

I am too willing to suffer in a relationship. I am too willing to accept "second best". I still don't say to myself, when a relationship is painful: "This doesn't feel good! I deserve better! It's not supposed to hurt to be in a relationship with someone who says he loves me!"

I am willing to pour my finances, time, help and love into someone who does not reciprocate with an equal willingness to "be there" for me. I am still willing to give and give and give and settle for the mere hope that, if I give enough, maybe some day the other person will also give mutually towards me. Consequently, selfish, demanding, emotionally unavailable people are drawn to me like a giant magnet.

I am too willing and too quick to accommodate, adapt or "flex" with what another person needs or wants. I have not, as yet, developed the skill to be honest about my true feelings and needs. I have not learned to put just as high a value on what I feel or need as I do on what another person feels or needs. As a result, I will attract people who are rigid, stubborn and, once again, extremely selfish.

I hesitate to be honest when I am uncomfortable or if I disagree with a person, out of fear of losing the relationship. This hesitation is an automatic recipe for disaster. It just about guarantees I will attract an unhealthy person. A whole, healthy person will not stick around, once he realizes I am not someone he can trust to be emotionally honest and "up front" with him! On the other hand, unhealthy people will love my reluctance to speak my mind. My inability to be up front about my honest feelings allows the other person in the relationship to be demanding, abusive, selfish and controlling, all with a minimum amount of hassles from me!

A final word of encouragement!

God used Psalm 103:1-5 to make some promises to me, a long time ago, when I first began my journey to be healed of the wounds from my past. Those promises express what He wants to do for every person who is struggling to overcome the cycle of abuse in his or her life.

"My child...
I have forgiven all of your sins!
I have healed all of your diseases!
I am the one who can also redeem your life from the pit you are in.

If you will let me...
I will crown you with My loving kindness and My compassion!
I will satisfy your years with good things.
I will renew your lost youth like the eagle!

Love,
Papa God"'

**The author of *A Trip To Freedom*
welcomes hearing from you.
She can be contacted at:**

Lighthouse of Hope Ministries
PMB #365
914 164th Street SE, #B-12
Mill Creek, Washington 98012

(425) 775-3904
www.lighthouse-of-hope.org
ruth@lighthouse-of-hope.org

To request additional copies of

A Trip To Freedom

Send $12 USA ($20 CDN) donation to:
Lighthouse of Hope Ministries
(See address above.)

***Discounts Available for
Quantity Orders and Ministries***